WELSH HYMNS AND THEIR TUNES

Their background and place in Welsh History and Culture

ALAN LUFF

Hope Publishing Company
CAROL STREAM, IL 60188

Stainer & Bell
LONDON

Dedication

"To Enid, who taught me my Welsh and to Ann, Gwilym, Robin and Hywel, our children, with whom I spoke and sang it"

CONTENTS

MAP OF WALES

Showing the counties as they were until 1973, and the most important places mentioned in the text. Many small towns and villages are named because of the association of a hymn writer or composer with them, or because a hymn tune is named after them.

Preface

On November 1st 1988 there was a great service in Westminster Abbey to commemorate 400 years of the Bible in Welsh and to give thanks for the *Welsh New Bible,* the first complete translation of the Bible since that of 1588. Those organizing the service from the side of the Abbey authorities had some difficulty in accepting the plans for the worship: they did not fit with what experience taught them would be successful in Westminster Abbey. On the day it became apparent why there was this difference. The English had not imagined what the Welsh had taken for granted, the great flood-tide of congregational singing that swept that service along.

The Welsh are proud of their hymns. They have done much to study the texts; less work has been done on the tunes. But although most of those who have undertaken this work are completely bilingual in English and Welsh, they have chosen to write about their hymns in Welsh. Especially when working on the texts this is entirely understandable, since they inevitably lose much in translation. But in reality it is the tunes that fascinate much of the hymn-singing world outside Wales, and they can be very properly discussed in English.

I am English by birth and upbringing. I was fortunate to have the opportunity and incentive to learn Welsh in my 20s and to become fluent by speaking it regularly in our home. In 1968 I moved to take charge of a parish in North Wales where there were four congregations to whom I ministered, two English and two Welsh. For eleven years therefore I lived alongside the Welsh hymns. I built up a warm working relationship with the chapels in the parish and sang hymns with their ministers and people. By a quite extraordinary turn of events I became chairman of the Bangor Diocesan Music Committee, the only committee in the Church in Wales to conduct its business entirely in Welsh. It is with this background that I have dared to do what the Welsh have been unwilling to do for themselves, that is to interpret their hymn culture to the world outside Wales.

In discussing the history of the Methodist Revival and of the hymn texts I have been largely dependent upon the Welsh scholars, some of whom I list below. Inevitably I have taken their work and shaped it, interpreted it and tried to put it in such a way that it can be understood by those without the background that the Welsh writers grew up with and take for granted. Since less work has been done on the tunes, it is fair to say that there is more of my own work and judgement in that part of the book. It is probably an advantage to the general reader that I have had to work my way into this culture myself from outside. Because of that I am aware of some of the things that need explaining, and particularly in the first two chapters I concentrate on providing this essential background. I trust that in giving what is in the end my own personal interpretation I have not proved false to those on whose labours I have depended.

The shape and proportions of the book speak for themselves. Everything leads to the tunes, and it is they that take pride of place. There are many more tunes, particularly from the great period of fifty years from about 1860-1910, than are given here, and strong cases could be made for the inclusion of many of them. But with the selection given here the reader will be able to make the acquaintance of a great hymn culture.

Of the writers in Welsh to whom I am most indebted I must mention R.T. Jenkins, who in the 1920s and 1930s wrote with elegance and passion on the 18th and 19th century; G.M. Roberts who in this generation has written extensively on the general history of the Revival, and brought together others to do the same; Derek Llwyd Morgan (whose major book of 1981 on the Revival is now available in English as *The Great Awakening):* Evan Isaac who wrote in the 1920s on the Hymn Writers of Wales; R.D. Griffiths who wrote the only book on the history of congregational singing in Wales (published 1948); Huw Williams who besides his two books on the hymntunes in the Welsh Methodist Hymn Book *Emynau a Thonau* continues to bring important details to light in his writings; and the writers of the *Dictionary of Welsh Biography down to 1940.* No one can touch on any aspect of Welsh Literature without debt to Thomas Parry's great work on the history of Welsh literature, or on the Welsh carols without recourse the work of Enid Roberts and D. Roy Saer. *The Bulletin of the Welsh Hymn Society* has produced much important material.

In English it is possible to give a more formal bibliography:

Wales is uniquely provided with *A Bibliography of Welsh Hymnody to 1960* by H. Turner Evans (Welsh Library Association, Caernarvon 1977). The short biographies are in English, but the extremely full lists of references in each case are almost invariably to Welsh books and articles.

There is a great deal of historical study of Wales in progress at the moment with a number of important series of general histories in progress. I am particularly indebted to Kenneth O. Morgan *Rebirth of a Nation — Wales 1880-1980* (Oxford University Press and University of Wales Press 1982). I have also found useful *A History of Wales 1485-1660* by Hugh Thomas and *A History of Wales 1660-1815* by E.D. Evans (both University of Wales Press, Cardiff 1972 and 1976; there is also a volume covering 1815-1906 by David Gareth Evans, 1989). *Modern Wales, a Concise History c. 1485-1979* by Gareth Elwyn Jones (Cambridge University Press 1984) is useful in dealing with the period topically rather than in a purely chronological manner.

The writings of Geoffrey F. Nuttall first aroused my interests in the first preachers of the Revival in Wales, in particular *Howel Harris 1714-1773, The Last Enthusiast* (Cardiff, University of Wales Press 1965), and *The Welsh Saints 1640-1660* (ibid. 1957).

The Oxford Book of Welsh Verse in English chosen by Gwyn Jones (Oxford University Press 1977) includes both translations and pieces originally written in English as does *The Penguin Book of Welsh Verse* edited by Anthony Conran.

There is a series of monographs, the *Writers of Wales* series, published by The University of Wales Press on behalf of the Welsh Arts Council. In it Glyn Tegai Hughes writes on William Williams, Pantycelyn, and A.M. Allchin on Ann Griffiths (This latter is reprinted with additions and a complete translation of all Ann's writings by Cowley Publications, Cambridge, Mass. under the title *Songs to her God*).

Uniquely among Welsh writers there is a great deal of writing on Ann Griffiths in English. A.M. Allchin discusses her in his three books *The World is a Wedding*, 1978, *The Kingdom of Love and Knowledge* 1979 and *The Dynamic of Tradition* 1981 (Dartman, Longman and Todd Ltd). As part of the celebration of the two hundredth anniversary of her birth in 1976 H.A. Hodges edited a book for the Church in Wales *Homage to Ann Griffiths* which included a translation of the seminal lecture of 1965 by Sanders Lewis on the literary aspect of Ann Griffiths and his own complete translation of her hymns. For the *Archivio Italiano* John Ryan produced *The Hymns of Ann Griffiths* (Ty ar y Graig 1980) which includes an annotated translation by himself and Robert O.F. Wynne of both the hymns and the letters.

There have been many small books of translations of Welsh Hymns, most now only to be picked up secondhand. Worth looking for still is the more substantial book by H. Elvet Lewis *Sweet Singers of Wales* (The Religious Tract Society, London c. 1890) with a considerable number of translations. Miss Jane Owen of Llanfairfechan, Gwynedd, has been the most assiduous and most successful translator of this generation, but her work has only appeared in Welsh journals; I am glad to be able to include some in this book and hope to see them collected at some time.

For those whose only knowledge of Welsh Poetry in English comes from the poems of Dylan Thomas, there can be recommended *Anglo-Welsh Poetry 1480-1980* edited by Raymond Garlick and Roland Mathias (Poetry Wales Press 1984). The ebullient variety of the contemporary writing there gives a greater insight, both pessimistic and optimistic, into the nature of Wales today than can many volumes of prose.

November 1989, Westminster Abbey, London

ACKNOWLEDGMENTS

The author and publishers gratefully acknowledge the kind permission to reproduce copyright material as follows:

Chapter 1

'So I fall in love, do I' and 'Nothing but a hovel now' translated by Rolfe Humphries, from *Nine Thorny Thickets: Selected Poems of Dafydd ap Gwilym* (1969), translated by Rolfe Humphries. Reprinted by permission of Kent State University.

Chapter 2

'Y bore glas', 'Mynd efo Dewi i Dywyn', 'Y Gwydd', 'Lisa Lân', and 'Awn i Fethlem' are reprinted by permission of The Welsh Folk Song Society (Cymdeithas Alawon Gwerin Cymru).

'Angelic hosts proclaimed him' and 'As Jesus Christ lay fast asleep' by Fred Pratt Green. Reprinted by permission of Stainer and Bell Ltd. and Hope Publishing Ltd.

'Wel dyma'r bore gorau i gyd'. Reprinted by permission of The Welsh Folk Museum, St. Fagan's, Cardiff.

'Old age never comes alone' translated by Anthony Conran. Reprinted by permission of the translator.

Chapter 3

The passage from Kenneth Morgan *Rebirth of a Nation – Wales 1880-1980* (1982 Oxford University Press/University of Wales Press). Reprinted by permission of Oxford University Press.

Chapter 4

The passage from Giraldus Cambrensis *The Description of Wales* translated by Lewis Thorpe. Reproduced by permission of Penguin Books Ltd.

Lines from 'A Christmas Revel' by Dafydd Bach ap Madog Wylaidd, translated by Joseph Clancy from *The Earliest Welsh*

Poetry (1970 Macmillan/St. Martin's Press). Reprinted by permission of the translator.

'The Resurrection and the Life' translated by M.J.H. Ellis. Reprinted by permission of the translator.

'Can I forget bright Eden's grace', 'Wondrous sight for men and angels', 'O might I gain faith's insight', 'O wonder always, happy bride', 'There he stands among the myrtles', and single lines by Ann Griffiths, translated by H.A. Hodges from *Homage to Ann Griffiths* (1976, Church in Wales). Reprinted by permission of Mrs. Vera J. Hodges.

'O wash me daily, wash me clean', 'All the morning stars were singing', 'He filleth heaven, he filleth earth', 'The blood that flowed upon the cross', 'Grant thy pure Spirit, Jesu, hear!', 'The source of my joy and my rapture' translated by Miss Jane Owen. Reprinted by permission of the translator.

'I gaze across the distant hills' translated by H. Idris Bell from *The Development of Welsh Poetry* (1936 Clarendon Press). Reprinted by permission of Idris Christopher Bell.

'Ride on, Jesus, all victorious' translated by the Rt. Revd. G.O. Williams. Reprinted by permission of the translator.

'Come, brethren, unite', 'Lord open my eyes to behold', 'In the waves and mighty waters', 'I also, like so many more', 'Existing in himself, before', 'My race beneath the sun' translated by H. Elvet Lewis from *Sweet Singers of Wales* (1889 The Religious Tract Society, London). Reprinted by permission of Piers Morgan.

'Far beyond time, beyond creation's dawn' translated by Edmund Tudor Owen. Reprinted by permission of the translator.

Extracts from 'Fugue for Ann Griffiths' by R.S.Thomas (*Welsh Airs* 1987, Seren Books). Reprinted by permission of the publisher.

'Though altogether against nature' translated by Robert O.F. Wynne and John Ryan from *The Hymns of Ann Griffiths, The Text in Welsh with a translation and a critical introduction* (1980 Ty ar y graig). Reprinted by permission of Dr. John Ryan OMI St. Mary's College, Abbey Road, Rhos on Sea, Colwyn Bay, Clwyd.

Chapter 5

CAERLLEON harmonized by David Evans. Reprinted by permission of Oxford University Press.

'How dark was the night of his coming' words by Fred Pratt Green. Reprinted by permission of Stainer and Bell Ltd. and Hope Publishing.

YR HEN DDARBI arranged by Alan Luff. Reprinted by permission of Stainer and Bell Ltd.

'Christ is the King! O friend rejoice!' by G.K.A. Bell. Reprinted from *Enlarged Songs of Praise* by permission of Oxford University Press.

GLAN GEIRIONYDD harmonized by David Evans. Reprinted by permission of Oxford University Press.

LLWYNBEDW by J.T. Rees. Reprinted by permission of Morfudd Rhys Clark.

CYMER by Lewis Davies. Reprinted by permission of Gwyn Lewis Davies.

RHYS by W.J. Davies. Copyright owner not traced.

EBENEZER by T.J. Williams. Reprinted by permission of Eluned V. Jones and Dilys Evans.

YN Y GLYN by David Evans. Reprinted by permission of Oxford University Press.

PENNANT by T. Osborne Roberts. Reprinted by permission of Mrs. E. Laura Hughes.

BRYN MYRDDIN by J. Morgan Nichols. Copyright owner not traced.

MAELOR and ARWELFA by John Hughes. Reprinted by permission of Mrs. Enid Arwel Hughes.

TYDI A RODDAIST by Arwel Hughes. Reprinted by permission of Mrs. Enid Arwel Hughes.

Translations to which no name of a translator is appended are by the Author. Permissions to reproduce should be sought from the publisher.

Chapter 1

WALES,
THE WELSH LANGUAGE
AND THE WELSH PEOPLE

Wales, the Welsh language and the Welsh People

Wales, the land and its people have for generations been something of a mystery and because of that an attraction to those beyond its borders. In many parts it is unspoilt. Its central uplands are wild and it is still possible to drive for many miles without seeing another living soul. The kite and the buzzard fly over it serenely. The mountains of northern Wales are not high by international standards. Snowdon, the highest, is a modest 3,000 feet, but the grandeur of the scenery entices many visitors, and the sheer rock faces of the area have made it a school for many of the greatest rock climbers in the world. The south has its mysteries too, founded in the tales of a short, tough people, whose menfolk spent their working days toiling in the coalmines and their leisure time cheering on their rugby teams with male-voice singing of legendary power and sweetness. Above all in this land the people sang hymns, and they sang them in Welsh.

This is the true heart of the mystery. Here is a tiny country, entirely part of the United Kingdom, under government from London in a way that Scotland has never been, which nevertheless not only preserves its own culture — every county of England has something distinctive about it, and about the way its native inhabitants speak and behave — but actually has its own language.

The land that preserves that language is largely mountainous and agriculturally poor. Britain has been overrun again and again by invading tribes and conquering nations. Before the Romans came the whole of the southern part of the island was the home of Celtic tribes, who themselves had been invaders at some unrecorded point in history. The Romans pushed out from their base in south-east England and made many incursions into Wales along the three routes which, because of the geography of the land, are still the main traffic routes from east to west. They moved along the north coast to Anglesey and set up a fortified camp just outside Caernarvon; they moved along the central river valley of the Severn and beyond; and they moved across the most fertile part of Wales the southern plain to the farthest point where now is St. David's. The Romans lived alongside the Celts everywhere, and reshaped their lives, but they did not destroy the language or the culture. When they left, the Romanized Britons were almost certainly the originals for the stories of King Arthur and his Knights that form such an important part of the earliest

Welsh literature. Arthur was famous for his stand against the next waves of invaders, the Germanic tribes from continental Europe, and it was in fighting against these that he lost his life. These invaders did push the Celts westward, confining them and their languages to the western and northern parts of the island. Finally the Normans came in 1066. They took their time over the conquest of Wales. They first established their warrior Lords along the borders, the so called Welsh Marches, and then took over the profitable farming land, particularly of the south. They made firm their rule, setting up the great castles which are still so much a feature of the land, but their way of life did not penetrate into the poor uplands and into the mountains. These parts retained a way of life distinctive of the people and of the land, and these are still the areas where the Welsh language survives, in Anglesey, Gwynedd, in the mountains of Powys and Meirionydd, and in the southwest corner, though even there the southern part of old Pembrokeshire, where the land is fertile, is heavily anglicized.

Apart from the industrial southeast of Wales, and a small area in northeast Wales, the land is largely given over to farming. It is true that the country has some mineral resources. Lead and the silver that is found with it, were mined from the days of the Romans in several parts of Wales. Gold was mined in North Wales and the work has been taken up many times since, but quantities have always been small. It has been traditional for royal wedding rings to be made from Welsh gold. Copper has been important in Wales from the 17th century, when the area around Neath in the south became important as a centre for the smelting of copper both locally mined and imported. From the late 18th century the emphasis shifted to the eastern part of Anglesey where the now desolate landscape of Mynydd Parys (Parys Mountain) is evidence of industrial activity especially at the time of the Napoleonic Wars. Likewise in the northwest there are slate and granite quarries which once exported large quantities of material for the building of the great industrial cities of England and for the paving of their roads with cobbles. Most of these are now abandoned, having brought more profit to their owners than to the workers, and having left behind them their industrial narrow-gauge railways which have in many cases been re-built by enthusiasts and are now run as tourist attractions as the little steam-trains of Wales. The industrial area of the southeast exists because of the iron that is found there. It was first smelted with wood and charcoal, then later with the coal that was found in abundance. The coal proved to be of a high quality and very suitable for use in steam engines, and in the final decades of the 19th century and the first decades of the 20th Wales was the provider of high-class steam coal to the navies of the world. The coal is, however, in narrow seams and hard to extract, and the prosperity of the region has proved fragile in this century.

Most of Wales remained and still is rural. The lowlands are fertile, but much of the land is mountainous and marginal for farming. It has been brought into use and again abandoned many times as farm prices have fluctuated, and upland Wales is scattered with abandoned farms and even whole villages because of this. On such land sheep farming can be practised, the sheep wandering the mountains all summer and being brought down to the lower ground to winter and for lambing, before they are sheared and sent off again to follow the old sheep tracks. The weaving of the very hard-wearing wool from these sheep was once an important cottage industry. Woollen mills, especially water-driven, gradually took over the industry in the 19th century. A number of these still survive, producing woollen goods in distinctive traditional patterns that are of interest in themselves and are a great attraction to tourists. In fact, since the last century, tourism has become the most important 'industry' in many parts of rural Wales, and the poor land pays better when planted with tents and caravans than with crops.

Because of the nature of the terrain and the lack of resources Wales is a land of small towns and villages with a decentralized culture. For example, the University of Wales is divided into four University Colleges, at Aberystwyth, Bangor, Cardiff and Swansea. The larger cities and towns of the south are becoming more important in national life, but Cardiff does not have the same importance to Wales as has London for England. It was not declared the capital of Wales until the 1970s. It has never been necessary to go to Cardiff to make one's mark in Wales. Thus it is no accident that many of the most important figures in Welsh life have attached to their personal name that of the small village, or even the farm or cottage, where they were born or resided in later life. It was from these small centers that they exerted their influence on the life of the nation.

This extra identification has been made necessary by the fact that so many Welsh people share the same surname — Jones,

Williams, Evans, Roberts, Owen, Davies. In fact the surname is a relatively late development in Wales. Men were known by their own given name followed by 'ap' (son of) and their father's name (e.g. Robert ap John). This usage gave rise to some of the other common Welsh surnames: thus 'ap Richard' became 'Prichard', 'ap Rhys' became 'Prys' or 'Prees' or 'Price', and 'ap Robert' 'Probert'. In other cases the father's name turned into one of the very common surnames: 'John' became 'Jones', 'David' became 'Davies' and so on. Today one of the most frustrating experiences can be trying find a number in a Welsh telephone directory. It is quite essential to have the address of the 'John Jones' that is being sought. This is exactly as it has always been, though in the past it was not the house number and the street that was given as the additional identification, but the village or the house or farm. A name that will often be met in these pages is that of William, one of whose ancestors must have been 'William' to give him the surname 'Williams', who lived most of his life at a farm called 'Pantycelyn', and was thus known as 'William Williams, Pantycelyn'. There is one further trick that the Welsh use. In many Welsh communities nicknames are common, and these become part of the name. Many communities therefore have their 'Thomas the Post'; Dylan Thomas' 'Dai Bread', and the other rich characters of 'Under Milk Wood' have names that can be matched from real life, such as 'Wil Jolly' who was William who was born at the pub 'The Jolly Herring'.

The Welsh Language

Welsh is a Celtic language, and the Welsh people themselves still show physical traces of their Celtic ancestry, despite the great mixture of people in the British Isles as a whole. The Welsh are the remnant of a once great people who spread right across Europe in the centuries before Christ. The names given them can be confusing, but the name of the branch which settled in Asia Minor gives the clue, that is the Galatians (to whose early Christian Church St. Paul wrote a letter). If the second 'a' of the name is removed it is easy to see how the name is linked with 'Celt'; if the first three letters are taken, it is clear how the name is linked with 'Gaul', the name by which the Romans knew the present day France and its inhabitants. The French today know Wales as 'Pays de Galles' and the Welsh know their land as 'Gwalia', from which is easily derived the English name 'Wales'. The Welsh themselves are more likely, however, to refer to themselves as 'Cymry' and the land as 'Cymru'; the language is always called 'Cymraeg'. 'Cymry' is a name that originally appeared in the 6th century for the Celtic peoples from Wales and from the Scottish Lowlands who were 'a band of brothers' united against the Saxons. The English are still called the 'Saison' by the Welsh as the Scots call them the 'Sassenachs'.

The Celts were not the simple barbaric Warriors that the Romans often portrayed. Archaeology reveals them as a highly artistic race whose metalwork was staggeringly beautiful. They valued the spoken word highly both in prose and verse. Thus nothing was written down in the earlier period. Not everything is lost from that early time however. In a society without writing the power of the memory, especially in professional speakers and reciters, is highly cultivated and we can be reasonably sure that some of the oral material from the early periods survived to be written down by later generations.

The Celtic languages that survive are the Irish Gaelic, the Scottish Gaelic, the Manx language (from the Isle of Man), Breton and Welsh. Cornish is now strictly a dead language, since the last native speaker died earlier this century, but it is enthusiastically studied by patriotic Cornishmen. Breton, Cornish and Welsh are from the Brythonig branch of the language and their speakers can understand one another to some extent. The others make up the Godelic branch, and the two branches cannot be understood by one another. All the surviving Celtic languages are under threat, especially now from the existence of the mass media which bring the majority language of the countries into every home. However in both Ireland and Wales there is much being done officially to encourage the language. According to the official census Welsh is now spoken by between 20% and 25% of the population. There is some vagueness since it is not clear exactly what the census figure means. It could be an underestimate, with many who understand Welsh reasonably well and even attend worship in Welsh excluding themselves on the census form because they find speaking Welsh difficult or cannot write it correctly; or it could be an overestimate if too much of this Welsh 'penumbra' is included. It would once have been true to say those who speak Welsh are an aging group. This remains true in that the stronghold of the language is in the Welsh chapels and they are reduced in many places to small groups of elderly people. On the other hand there is growing up a younger generation who are not only Welsh speakers but eagerly, even militantly so. They are building a modern culture in Welsh. In certain parts of Wales, Welsh remains the normal language of everyday life. Many families outside these areas speak Welsh in the home, worship in a Welsh chapel or church and support the activities of a local Welsh society. This is true not only in the anglicized parts of Wales but in England and even overseas.

The language is a difficult one to learn for those used only to those languages related to English. The basic structure of English is Germanic through Anglo-Saxon, but much has come into the language from latin sources, both directly and through Norman-French. Welsh, while still one of the Indo-European group of languages has a distinctive Celtic structure. There are also sounds unique to the language, the 'll' sound and the 'u' as it is pronounced in North Wales. The vowels are pure 'continental' sounds, not the permanently shifting vowels of English in all its forms. The spelling is entirely regular and phonetic, so that even if the language itself presents problems, the names of people and places can be pronounced correctly once the rules are known.

The literature that has grown up in this language is a strong one and has a long, continuous history. The few poems from the 7th century that survive are difficult for the modern reader but are recognizably Welsh, whereas English as we know it did not develop for a further 500 years. In the ancient Welsh society the great houses of the land, and even some lesser families, gave protection and a livelihood to the bards, the poet-musicians. The duty of these bards was to recite the ancient poetic stories and to sing the praises of God, of the Saints and of their patrons. This they did in close-packed verse of great obscurity during the years preceding and including the conquest of Wales by Edward I of England near the end of the 13th century. One writer has said of them: "What these poets give is not so much a meaning as clues to a meaning". In the 14th century there developed a less archaic style, though one still tightly controlled by a most complicated scheme of rime and alliteration. The great master of the style was Dafydd ap Gwilym, who turned his great lyric gifts to honouring the women he loved as well to the Madonna. He could mock himself:

So I fall in love, I do,
Every day, with one or two,
Get no closer, any day,
Than an arrow's length away.

But he is most distinctly himself in poetry that combines love with an acute observation of nature:

Nothing but a hovel now
Between the moorland and meadow,
Once the owners saw in you
A comely cottage, bright, new,
Now roof, rafters, ridge-pole, all
Broken down by a broken wall.

A day of delight was once there
For me, long ago, no care
When I had a glimpse of her
Fair in an ingle-corner.
Besides each other we lay
In the delight of that day.

(translations by Rolfe Humphries)

So began a long tradition of semi-popular religious poetry centred on the Cross taking as its theme the intensity of Christ's sufferings for us. In the 14th century the prose writers too were concerned to expound the Christian faith in their native tongue. But this, like the poetry, was largely for the benefit of wealthy patrons, though some of it may have been intended for the parish clergy to use in their teaching of the faith to their people. The great Latin hymns were translated at various periods — the 'Veni Creator' and the 'Salve Regina' for example. There is also a long history of popularity for a Welsh 'Lorica' or 'Breastplate', the Hymn of the Martyr Curig ('St. Patrick's Breastplate' is an Irish hymn of this kind), but the foundations of Welsh hymnody are not to be found here.

The Welsh are aware of the antiquity of their language and of the literature, especially of the poetry. For them poetry is not the strange fancy of an elite few but a part of daily life. The Royal National Eisteddfod is more concerned with literature than with music, the two great occasions of the week being the ceremonies of the Chairing of the Bard and of the Crowning of the Bard, the winners in the two major poetry competitions. There are many lesser competitions in Wales, but all, even the Eisteddfod in the humblest local chapel, will have its competition for the writing of some form of verse, often an 'englyn', a tight-packed, epigrammatic form with strict rules, going back to the Middle Ages. It is difficult to translate but something of the feel is given in:

> 'Old age never comes alone' – it brings sighs
>   With it, and complaining,
> And now a long lack of sleep,
> And, soon enough, long slumber.
> > *(John Morris-Jones 1884-1929,*
> > *trans. Anthony Conran)*

It has rightly been pointed out that prose writing comes from a more developed society than poetry. Thus there have been arid periods in the writing of Welsh prose. There was a long gap after the translation of the Bible into Welsh in the 16th century. The growing self-awareness of the 19th century is expressed in an awakening both of mature poetry and later of prose. There is no tradition of Welsh novel writing. The 'novels' of Daniel Owen in the 19th century are episodic in nature, though the picture they give of contemporary life centred on church and chapel is richly comic. Novels have been written in this century, but the short story is still stronger in Welsh than the novel. It could be that this generation is producing the developments that will lead to a school of novel writers. Until the 1950s there was a clear distinction between literary and colloquial Welsh. It was not that the colloquial was a slipshod version of the literary language; each was to be used in its proper context and was correct there. Since that time there has been a growing movement to have first the characters in novels speak and think as they really do, and then to tell the story in the same colloquial Welsh. This move was naturally shocking at first but it has brought fresh strength to short stories and novels. The same period has seen a great growth in the Welsh Theatre. The poets are also being influenced by the same development. Those who fight to preserve the Welsh language are fighting to preserve not only an important literary tradition, but a culture that has still a great deal of life and can be seen even now to be moving into a new period. It is a culture wholly different from the English, even though the bilingual Welshman may move with ease between the two languages.

Although the great fascination of Wales in one respect is that it preserves this ancient language and still uses it for both daily life and for culture it would be wrong to suggest that it is impossible to approach the Welsh without a knowledge of that language. There has grown up in this century a strong Anglo-Welsh literature, that is, a literature written in English by Welshmen. It has been at times derided by those who use Welsh as when Saunders Lewis, the greatest poet in Welsh of his generation, said of Dylan Thomas that he was a fine young poet but lost to the English. No one who reads his poetry and short stories, to say nothing of 'Under Milk Wood', will wish to say that he was anything but Welsh. But there were and are others. Among the novelists there are John Cowper Powys and Richard Hughes. Perhaps the finest poet writing in English in the second half of the century is R.S. Thomas, a clergyman of the Church in Wales, whose stature is such that he seems to speak from Wales to the world.

Chapter 2

THE MUSIC
OF THE WELSH

The Music of the Welsh

The Hymn has become the folk-song of the Welsh. For those who attend chapel or church (and for many of those who do not) the substance of their musical thought is provided by hymns. When Welsh people gather, they are still likely at some stage to sing hymns, which to an outsider may seem to grow more intense, mournful even, as the evening wears on and the singers begin really to enjoy themselves. A school or club group returning from an outing will sing hymns in the coach on the way home. The sound of the Welsh supporters singing hymns at the rugby matches in the national stadium at Cardiff Arms Park is legendary. Choirs — particularly male choirs — include arrangements of hymns in their concert repertoire.

But there is a rich inheritance of 'folk-song' in the more widely accepted sense of traditional music, handed down by an oral tradition. That it had gone underground and has had to be rather self-consciously revived in many quarters is largely due to the triumph of the Evangelical Revival. Chapel culture discouraged church members from having anything to do with such ungodly pastimes as dancing and the singing of secular songs.

The structure of the folk tradition in Wales is rather different from that in England. It is useful to recognize this since it does impinge on hymn singing both within and outside Wales.

There are early references to two important musical instruments in Wales. The 'Crwth' (sometimes called the 'Crowd', the shape of which in earlier times is debated), has evolved as a bowed stringed instrument, usually with supporting shoulders for the neck of the instrument. But the harp is undisputed as the national instrument with its associations with the recitation of poetry by the bards. In the early and medieval periods the courts of local princes and nobles had their bards and minstrels. The chief musician-poet (Pencerdd) was in the ancient codes of laws and customs allotted an important position at court. While the sound of the music of these courts cannot be recovered, they undoubtedly contributed to the heritage of music that can now be met in Wales.

By far the best known Welsh melodies (other than the hymn tunes) are the harp melodies, and for many this has been the sum and end of Welsh folk music. These melodies were made known outside Wales by a succession of harpists who became very popular in England in the 17th, 18th and 19th centuries. In 1742 John

26

Parry (?1710-1820), the blind harpist, published *Ancient British Music*, with a second volume in 1745, being assisted in the arrangements by Evan Williams (1710-some time before 1777). In 1781 he published *British Harmony*, a much better selection of melodies. In 1784 Edward Jones (1752-1824, known as 'Bardd y Brenin — The King's Bard') published *Relicks of the Welsh Bards*: the 1794 reprint contained many additional items. These were melodies mainly of Welsh origin, some of them published with variations in the fashion of the time. The earlier Welsh harpists played the 'triple harp', a form of the instrument in which there were three rows of strings, the outer rows tuned in unison and the inner row giving the semitones to make a full chromatic scale possible. Later Welsh harpers began to take up the continental pedal harp. The instrument has had a clear influence on the melodies, however ancient in origin many of them may be. Most of these melodies are in the modern major and minor keys. The harp plays chords easily and the melodies are built strongly around notes of the basic chords of the key, tonic, dominant and sub-dominant. The well-known *Ash Grove* makes this quite clear.

THE ASH GROVE (LLWYN ONN)   Form of melody as in *Gems of Welsh Melody*
John Owen (Owain Alaw) 1873

The meters of the tunes tend to be quite regular, in the usual duple, quadruple, triple and compound times. This might, taken together, seem a recipe for dullness, or at least for a music assimilated to the broad pattern of 18th and 19th century music as a whole. The distinctive Welsh character of many of these melodies makes it credible that they have a long history, though almost certainly not in the exact form in which we know them today. For example, the fine melody *Morfa Rhuddlan* (The Rhuddlan Marsh) is said to have been composed on the occasion of the defeat of Caradoc in 795, but must have undergone many changes since then.

MORFA RHUDDLAN
(RHUDDLAN MARSH)

Form of melody as in *Gems of Welsh Melody*
John Owen (Owain Alaw) 1873

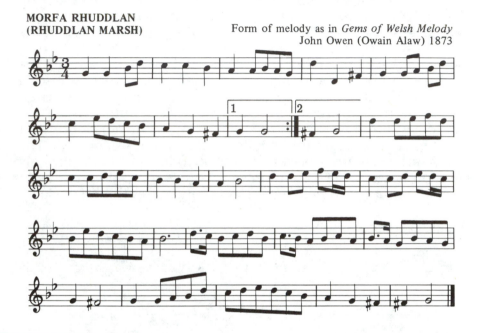

Other harp melodies that have become world famous are *Men of Harlech, David of the White Rock* and *All through the night.*

It may seem surprising that these tunes have all been referred to as instrumental pieces, but that is how they have come down to us. John Parry and Evan Williams clearly thought at some stage of supplying the words to the tunes that they published. It is most sad that they did not, since for the most part the original words have not survived for these tunes. The melodies were recovered for later singers by the activity in the 19th century of a number of very skilful versifiers who wrote fresh words for them. John Ceiriog Hughes (1832-1887) was the most popular of these and his themes, particularly of wistful love and longing for home, with much reference to the hills and valleys of Wales, have

28

become identified with this kind of song. The English words associated with these tunes are often quite different from the best known Welsh words, but since neither the English or the Welsh words are those originally associated with the tune this should cause no concern. For example the *Ash Grove* is sung in English to a celebration of the delights of the country lover; in Welsh it is called *Llwyn Onn* and is a tragic story of an accidental shooting while out hunting with the bow.

Singing words in this way to the melodies associated with the harp is known in South Wales as *Canu Penillion* (Singing Verses). The same name is given in North Wales to a different vocal tradition associated with the harp melodies, that is also known as *Cerdd Dant* (literally 'the music of the string'). Though originating in North Wales this traditional form of singing can now be heard all over Wales. In it the harp plays a traditional melody over which the voice enters singing a countermelody. No slurred notes are allowed and the voice should enter after the harp has begun but end exactly with it. In the final analysis, however, this is a *tour de force* for the verse writer rather than the singer, since the verses should be in one of the 24 traditional metres of Welsh poetry with their internal rimes and intricate patterns of multiple alliteration. In most penillion singing that is heard today this work of composition has been done beforehand, and for the most part the pieces are sung by a choir of men's or women's voices whether in unison or in parts. The competitions for penillion singing are largely of this nature. This runs entirely contrary however to the origin of the form which is essentially *ex tempore*. At the old eisteddfodau the harp would play over once one of a fairly wide range of tunes used for this purpose and on the second time round the singer had to enter, improvising words and countermelody. The experienced performer no doubt had a mind well stocked with turns of verbal and musical phrase, but with the harpist embroidering the melody (though one must assume retaining the conventional harmonic structure of the accompaniment) there was the element of a gladiatorial contest in music. Ideally there would be also in the words some personal or contemporary reference. Good intonation and clear diction remain more important to this form when performed as a solo than conventionally beautiful singing. Many Welsh harpists today perform in this way to their own playing, but usually the pieces are pre-composed. There has been a revival in some quarters of the competitive *ex tempore* element.

The folk-song proper is different again from the singing associated with the harp. For a long time it was assumed in Wales as in England that there was nothing worth the attention of the cultivated musician in the everyday singing of ordinary people. But there is — or perhaps, rather, was — a great treasury here. Some songs were collected by the harpists in the 18th century and brought by them into conformity with major and minor scales. On the other hand, John Jenkins, Vicar of Kerry (1770-1829, known as Ifor Ceri), in making an important collection in the early 19th century noted some of the problems of key and intonation that he met when trying to write them down. Other important collections of folk dances and songs were made in the last century, particularly important being the work of Maria Jane Williams of Aberpergwm (1795-1873) who won the first prize at the National Eisteddfod of 1838 for a collection of unpublished Welsh traditional songs, and continued her valuable work of collecting and publishing for many years. But the real understanding of this tradition of vocal folk music does not go back earlier than the beginning of this century and went in parallel with the work going on at the same time in England. This led to the founding of the Welsh Folk Song Society and the publication of a large amount of material in its Journal. There was by then a greater awareness of the fact that the older music, including folk-songs, used modes other than major and minor. The problems of intonation noted by Jenkins of Kerry were followed up and early recording techniques proved what earlier collectors had tried to put on paper, that some songs were being sung by traditional singers with a tuning that placed the all important third and seventh degrees of the scale too sharp to be minor and too flat to be major.

Many of the songs that were collected are hauntingly beautiful, as is this version of *Y bore glas.*

Y BORE GLAS

Pan o'wn i ar fo - re-ddydd, Ar las_ wyn y dydd,_ Yn rho-dio glâs y _

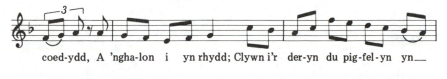

coed-ydd, A 'ngha-lon i yn rhydd; Clywn i'r der-yn du pig-fel-yn yn__

can-u yn y dyff-ryn A__ min-nau'n ei__ serch-u yn y gwŷdd.

As in most folk-song traditions the songs may have a nonsense refrain, as in this song from Barmouth which tells of a journey and what was eaten and drunk on the way.

WRTH FYND EFO DEIO I DYWYN (Going with Deio to Towyn)

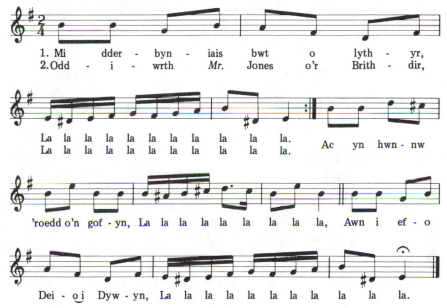

1. Mi   dder - byn - iais   bwt   o   lyth - yr,
2. Odd - i - wrth   *Mr.* Jones   o'r   Brith - dir,

La la la la la la la la   la   la   la.
La la la la la la la la   la   la   la.   Ac   yn   hwn - nw

'roedd o'n gof - yn, La la la la la   la   la   la la,   Awn   i   ef - o

Dei - o i Dyw - yn, La la la la la   la   la la   la   la   la.

While it is not true that the Welsh hymn tunes are mainly in the minor key, it is true that many Welsh folk-songs have a minor flavour, being in fact in the dorian mode. *Y Gwŷdd* comes from the collection by Maria Jane Williams.

Y GWŶDD (The Loom)

Pan oedd wn ar frig_ nos-waith Yn y_gwŷdd, Yn y_ gwŷdd,_ Yn

gweith - io 'nghrefft mewn_go baith, Yn_ y_ gwŷdd, Yn_ y_gwŷdd:

Medd - yl - iais wrth fy hun-an Na wydd wn pa mor fu - an, Er

dwys-ed oedd fy am-can, Yn y_ gwŷdd, Yn_ y_ gwŷdd,_ Pan

gawn ym - ad - o'r_ cyf - an, Yn y_gwŷdd, Yn_ y_gwŷdd.

There are a number of versions of *Lisa Lân* (Fair Liza), but this one, with the major third but the insistence on the flattened seventh, is particularly haunting.

LISA LÂN (Fair Lisa)

1. Bûm yn dy gar - u law - er gwaith, Do, law - er awr mewn mwyn-der

maith; Bûm yn dy gus - an - u, Li - sa gêl, Yr oedd dy gwm-ni'n well na'r mêl.

There are many beautiful children's songs, nursery rimes and lullabies. *Gee ceffyl bach* is sung bouncing the child up and down on the knee.

GEE CEFFYL BACH

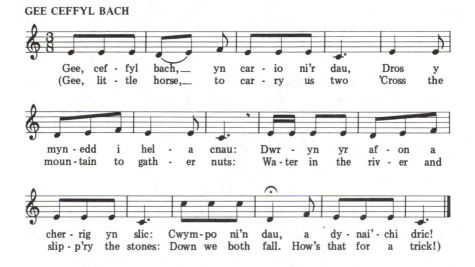

Gee, cef - fyl bach,— yn car - io ni'r dau, Dros y
(Gee, lit - tle horse,— to car - ry us two 'Cross the

myn - edd i hel - a cnau: Dwr - yn yr af - on a
moun - tain to gath - er nuts: Wa - ter in the riv - er and

cher - rig yn slic: Cwym-po ni'n dau, a dy - nai' - chi dric!
slip - p'ry the stones: Down we both fall. How's that for a trick!)

This is a true lullaby, which really does lull the child to sleep:

CYSGA DI

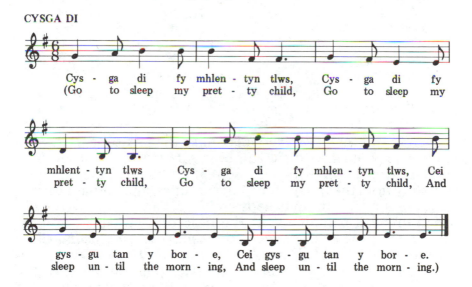

Cys - ga di fy mhlen - tyn tlws, Cys - ga di fy
(Go to sleep my pret - ty child, Go to sleep my

mhlent - tyn tlws Cys - ga di fy mhlen - tyn tlws, Cei
pret - ty child, Go to sleep my pret - ty child, And

gys - gu tan y bor - e, Cei gys - gu tan y bor - e.
sleep un - til the morn - ing, And sleep un - til the morn - ing.)

This by no means exhausts the repertoire or even the various types of Welsh folk-song. Unlike the conscious efforts by Vaughan Williams and his followers in the field of English folk song, the use made of these tunes in Welsh hymn singing has been extremely small. The reader is therefore left to explore this repertoire for its own sake.

Carols

The Carol needs separate treatment in Welsh, unlike the traditional Carol in English where it is very much part of the main body of folk-song. There are some few carols which do appear to belong to that folk-song tradition; *Awn i Fethlem* is among the very few that move like a folk-song:

AWN I FETHLEM

Even in this case, however, it is unlike the folk-song in that we know who wrote the words. This brings it into line with the carol and ballad tradition, which is essentially a literary phenomenon. Certainly from the 17th to the 19th centuries, and perhaps earlier, local poets were writing ballads and carols and many were published in small pamphlets. At the head of each ballad or carol stands the name of the meter, for example *Mesur: Mentra Gwen* (Measure or Meter: Venture Gwen), or *Mesur: Hir oes i Fair* (Measure: Long live Mary). Some of the later publications give the tunes all-together at the beginning or end of the pamphlet with the name of the *Mesur* at the head of each tune. Nicholas Bennett (1823-99) published 500 of these tunes in 1896 in two volumes entitled *Alawon fy Ngwlad* (Melodies of my Country). Valuable though this collection is, the tunes do not appear there in a very vocal form. For this it is necessary to examine the manuscript collections of tunes where, among the mixture of hymn tunes and short anthems, is to be found from time to time 'Mesur Carol', with the name of the measure and the tune much as it must have been sung. The names of the tunes have nothing to do with the content of the ballad or carol, any more than does the name of most hymn tunes. Many of the names are English, for example *Greece and Troy, Charity Mistress, Black-eyed Susan,* or can be traced to an English original; for example *Jermin Cloi* is *Charming Chloe.* There is a great uncertainty about the origin of most of these tunes, though some can be traced, usually to the theatres and streets of 17th century London. There was certainly a mode of transport for these tunes through the cattle drovers who bought cattle in Wales and drove them across to the English markets and were well known for their music.

The majority of the tunes are dull, mere vehicles for the all important words. There are however some striking tunes among them. There are well over a hundred measures or meters and often many tunes belong to each. One of the most fruitful in fine tunes is *Mentra Gwen.* Here are three of them: the first is a well known ballad by the 19th century Welsh Poet Ceiriog; he chose to use 'Mentra Gwen' (Venture, Gwen) as a refrain, and it is clear that the meter has a three syllable refrain; his version, however, is entirely his own and has nothing to do with any traditional 'folk' version. (This particular tune was printed in a hymnbook of 1840 but did not survive into later use as a hymntune.) The second is a strong, popular carol. The third is the form of a tune noted in a 19th century manuscript in North Wales, which also appears in both major and minor versions and in a more square rhythm as the hymntune TWRGWYN. It is interesting that the meter is the same as that of the American Folk Hymn *Wondrous Love.*

MENTRA GWEN

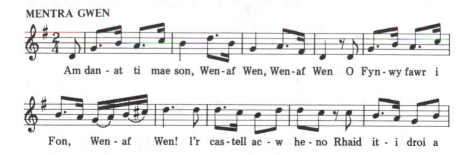

Am dan - at ti mae son, Wen-af Wen, Wen-af Wen O Fyn-wy fawr i

Fon, Wen - af Wen! I'r cas-tell ac - w he - no Rhaid it - i droi a

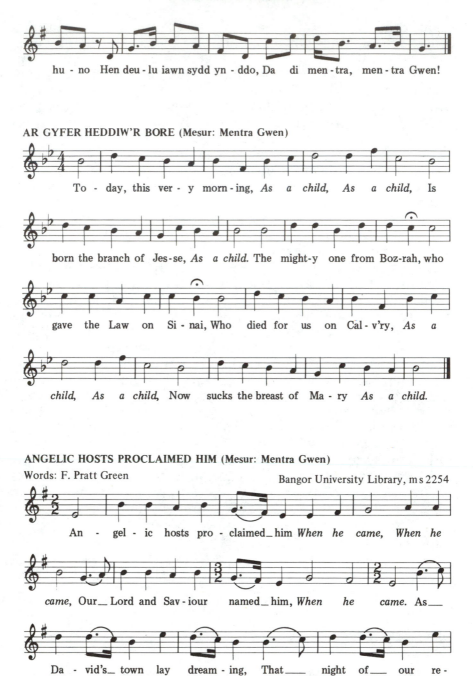

hu - no Hen deu - lu iawn sydd yn - ddo, Da di men - tra, men - tra Gwen!

AR GYFER HEDDIW'R BORE (Mesur: Mentra Gwen)

To - day, this ver - y morn - ing, *As a child, As a child,* Is

born the branch of Jes - se, *As a child.* The might-y one from Boz-rah, who

gave the Law on Si - nai, Who died for us on Cal - v'ry, *As a*

child, As a child, Now sucks the breast of Ma - ry *As a child.*

ANGELIC HOSTS PROCLAIMED HIM (Mesur: Mentra Gwen)

Words: F. Pratt Green

An - gel - ic hosts pro - claimed__ him *When he came, When he*

came, Our__ Lord and Sav - iour named__ him, *When he came.* As__

Da - vid's__ town lay dream - ing, That____ night of__ our re -

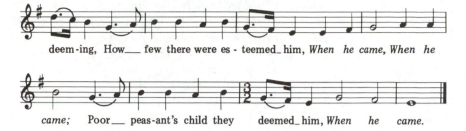

deem-ing, How___ few there were es - teemed_ him, *When he came, When he*

came;   Poor___ peas-ant's child they   deemed_ him, *When   he   came.*

The Welsh Carol is a field that has been little explored musically. Few of them are available in practical modern editions. Most of the studies have been on the words and on the interesting customs associated with the singing of the carols. The Welsh Folk Museum at St. Fagan near Cardiff has recorded the *Plygain* (Matins) ceremonies at which these carols are still sung. In its original form groups of singers, in the purest form of the tradition three or four men only and usually related to each other, would meet in secret in the weeks before Christmas to practise a number of traditional carols. These would be from their own manuscript books carefully preserved within the family, and the musical arrangements, crude but often effective, would be the property of that group. On Christmas Eve the group would spend the whole night moving from farm to farm, singing their carols and receiving refreshment. Very early on Christmas morning the different groups would gather at the Parish Church for Matins (Plygain). After the saying of the service the meeting was declared open and one by one groups and individuals would take the floor and sing their carols. When all the groups wishing to sing had sung once the first sang again each following the next in the order as before, and so on over and over again, the sole rule being that no two groups sang the same carol. Hence, after each round a number of groups would drop out, their carols having been already sung, albeit in another group's version. When all had sung themselves out the Parish Clerk would announce the Breakfast Carol, often peculiar to that Parish, and all the singers would go to the Vestry for refreshments. The custom survives in certain parts of Wales, but not as an early morning service. It is now held in Chapels as well as in Parish Churches, usually in the evening, though it is still known as the 'Plygain'. There are still groups who sing in the traditional manner in their own versions of the melodies. A small number of these arrangements have been published. This example is transcribed from a recording made by the Welsh Folk Museum's Department of Oral Tradition. The singers were three Williams brothers from Denbighshire who called themselves the *Parti Fronheulog*. The melody is one of the finest in the carol repertoire and is in the *Mesur: Ffarwel Ned Puw* (Farewell Ned Pugh). They sang words by a 19th century poet. The words given here were written for another version of the melody that appears in *Llyfr Carolau Deiniol* (1974 *The St. Deiniol Carol Book*). The arrangement will have been largely the responsibility of the singers, though based on the long tradition of which they are part.

AS JESUS CHRIST LAY FAST ASLEEP (Mesur: Ffarwel Ned Puw)
Words: F. Pratt Green

BARITONE

1. As Je - sus Christ_ lay fast_ a - sleep_And bed - ded in __ a man - ger,
2. Some sim-ple shep - herds left_ their sheep_To find_the heaven-ly strang-er.

TENOR

The Morn-ing Star_that shone_so bright_On trav - el - lers_ be night-ed Their

foot-steps guid-ed to_ the place_where, kneel-ing, they_ re - cit-ed

TENOR

1. For joy of the Boy we will sing you this car - ol, Though scratch-y our
2. Though sheep may be stu-pid, they know they must fol-low, The shep-herd who

BARITONE (melody)

1. For joy of the Boy we will sing you this car - ol, Though scratch-y our
2. Though sheep may be stu-pid, they know they must fol-low, The shep-herd who

BASS

1. For joy of the Boy we will sing you this car - ol, Though scratch-y our
2. Though sheep may be stu-pid, they know they must fol-low, The shep-herd who

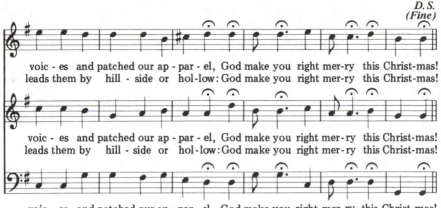

voic - es and patched our ap - par - el, God make you right mer-ry this Christ-mas!
leads them by hill - side or hol-low: God make you right mer-ry this Christ-mas!

There is also the custom of the *Mari Lwyd*. The origin of the name (which means 'Grey Mary') is unclear. In this predominantly South Wales custom there is a group of carol singers or 'mummers' one of whom is the 'Mari Lwyd', wearing a horse-head mask and covered in a sheet or long robe. They arrive at a house and start to sing. Those inside the house must reply in impromptu verses until one side breaks down. If that side is the one in the house then the doors must be opened and the *Mari Lwyd* party given refreshments. To be understood this custom has to be set in a culture where even now poetry in the old strict meters is appreciated and where there are many poetry competitions at the local eisteddfodau. There has even been a popular Welsh language television programme "Ymryson y Beirdd" (Competition of the Poets) in which week by week teams competed against each other in impromtu verse composition. An English verse associated with the *Mari Lwyd* has been preserved in the Gower Peninsula at Rhossili:

> Come open wide to us your door,
> We've come over field and ditch and
>   moor
> To wish you joy this Christmas tide,
> And eat your pudding by your leave,
> As we have done in years gone by,
> And hope to do so until we die.

Come Mrs — open your door
And let us have some food,
For the weather is cold and we must have   more.

A note adds that this is sung along with the traditional Welsh verses and goes along with the asking of riddles. Although the *Mari Lwyd* is now associated with Christmas it is clearly very ancient and probably pagan, connected with many other horse ceremonies and superstitions.

Welsh Composers

It is more difficult to deal with the composition of music in Wales than with its folk music, since the value placed on a composer within Wales does not necessarily correspond with his place upon the international scene. For a long time Wales was a backward country in this art. There was no opportunity to receive a musical education. Until the last decade of the 18th century there was no publication that set out the elements of music in Welsh. In the medieval period there had been patronage from the princes and lords for their bards and harpers, but this did not continue. The Welsh aristocracy did not maintain elaborate chapels with attendant musicians; the Welsh cathedrals were poor; there was no Welsh university; as a result there were no institutions able to sustain choral foundations such as those that nurtured so many English musicians. Thus until the 19th century there was not the cultural setting in which the composer of anything but folk-songs and hymntunes could flourish. As the Eisteddfod developed the glee became the largest musical form for which there were competitions. John Owen (1821-1883), John Ambrose Lloyd (1815-1874), Edward Stephen (1822-1885) all wrote songs, some anthems and cantatas, and Lloyd and Stephen each an oratorio. These were pioneers whose influence was greater than their lasting contribution. The next generation were better craftsmen. David Emlyn Evans (1843-1913) was a figure of great importance especially in the choral music of his day and in musical education. Joseph Parry (1841-1903) was the first Welsh composer to have a thorough professional education in music and was quite the best and most popular Welsh composer of his day. He taught most of the leading Welsh musicians of the next generation and was prolific in his output of oratorios, cantatas, operas, symphonies and smaller works, hardly any of which are heard today. David Jenkins (1848-1915) was the only other important figure of that generation, but again his work does not live on. (All these composers were important in the development of the Welsh hymntune and receive greater notice in ch 5.)

There was from the mid-nineteenth century a market for straightforward songs with piano accompaniment, and a number of composers wrote such songs, some of which are still performed. David Pughe Evans (1866-1907), R.S.Hughes (1855-1893) and William Davies (1859-1907) made their best contributions in this field. They have come under criticism for their poor taste in words. Later composers have been more careful in this respect, and have developed the accompaniments of their songs to be a more important part of the whole. The most important names are: David Vaughan Jones, Bradwen Jones, W. Albert Williams, Haydn Morris, David de Lloyd, J. Morgan Lloyd and E.T.Davies. The early death of Morfydd Llwyn Owen (1891-1918), a woman of prodigious talent was a tragedy for Welsh music.

Of the composers who came to be known by the middle of the 20th century, Arwel Hughes (1909-1988) is best known for his cantata *Dewi Sant*. Grace Williams (1906-77) was probably the most important figure of her generation, writing in a much more advanced idiom than anyone yet named, and waiting long for recognition. Her most important output was for orchestra and for orchestra and voices: she wrote one opera. Daniel Jones is the senior composer still writing (b 1912), with a large output of symphonies and other major works. The two leading figures who came to maturity after the Second World War are Alan Hoddinott (b 1929) and William Mathias (b 1934). They are conservative in their idiom by comparison with many composers of their generation outside Wales and the younger generation in Wales. There are aspects of their music which is recognizably Welsh but they enjoy international as well as Welsh appeal.

There are in Wales many younger composers of high talent. They are often trapped by their desire to be Welsh and to write music that springs from within their Welshness on the one side and on the other by their inability get a hearing either in England or Wales. In Wales their 'modern' idioms are not easily accepted in a largely rural and culturally conservative community: in London, where such music from all over the rest of the world is widely performed, they are thought to have a natural platform in Wales and are passed over on that account, especially by the B.B.C., the major patron of contemporary music. Thus many Welsh composers still wait to be given a proper place both in their own land and in the the current international world of music.

The Land of Song

Welsh musical life in general is in a period of transition. The choral tradition, built on the use of Tonic Sol-fa, which flourished up to the middle of this century has now dwindled. Whereas every large village once had its choral society, now these are few. Those that remain are much more enterprising than their predecessors however, who were all too often content with an unrelieved diet of Handel and Mendelssohn. A place is being found for the highly skilled small choir where once only the large oratorio choir was found. There are still large male choirs, and where these flourish it is often difficult to recruit men for the mixed choirs, despite the fact that there is no comparison between the repertoire available to the two kinds of choir. The male choirs generate intense enthusiasm and loyalty. They often meet three times a week to learn their music by rote and to commit it to memory. The best of the large male choirs provide a truly thrilling sound. They are very much a part of Welsh musical life, though their existence does tend to inhibit change.

The tradition of singing in Wales has been fostered from an early age by excellent work in the schools. There is now a much greater emphasis on instrumental teaching, leading to good school orchestras, through local youth orchestras to a fine National Youth Orchestra. This has led to a slight tendency for the school choir to take second place.

There are many music festivals up and down the country which bring performers of international reputation to local audiences. The B.B.C. Welsh Symphony Orchestra tours regularly, but, like other touring orchestras, with a very repetitive repertoire of popular classics since that is what fills halls in thinly populated areas.

At the peak of Welsh musical attainment is the Welsh National Opera. It has its headquarters in Cardiff, but its following is now worldwide. It draws leading principals, conductors and designers from all over the world, but its backbone is still a stream of fine Welsh singers. Here alone in Wales truly contemporary music has an accepted place. Exciting modern operas are often performed. Contemporary Welsh composers have written operas, though none have remained in the repertoire. Wales has taken Grand Opera to its heart. Whereas in an earlier generation aspiring local singers would work at solos from the oratorios, now they sing the great operatic arias, and their ambition is to sing for the Welsh National Opera. In the last century many boys were called 'Handel' or 'Haydn': in the latter years of the 20th century, there must be many parents tempted to name their boys 'Verdi'.

Wales has often been called a great musical nation. The Welsh phrase *Gwlad y Gân* (The Land of Song) is more accurate.

The Eisteddfod

The word 'eisteddfod' is one of the few Welsh words that has been borrowed by the world at large (and even pronounced reasonably correctly in the process). In current usage it denotes a competitive musical festival, with which concerts may be associated.

Its origin is quite different. The root of the word is 'eistedd', meaning 'to sit'. So it was in origin a 'sitting down', a 'session', at which bards, that is, poet-musicians gathered. They went into session to confer the status of 'bard' on those qualified and, like any guild of craftsmen, to establish the rules of their craft. There were poetical and musical competitions in which the masters demonstrated their skills, but the serious business was that of the organizing of the craft and its work. The 16th century *eisteddfodau* (the plural of 'eisteddfod') looked back to Grufudd ap Cynan (d. 1137) who revised and revitalized certain poetic forms by calling an *eisteddfod*, and to an *eisteddfod* summoned by Lord Rhys ap Grufydd in 1176. In the 16th century it is clear that *eisteddfodau* were held from time to time, by royal commission, and under the immediate patronage of Welsh noblemen and leading poets. The most famous of these historic *eisteddfodau* were that of Carmarthen in 1450 (which was actually called an *eisteddfod*, unlike some of the earlier gatherings), and those of Caerwys in 1523 and 1568.

It is difficult to believe that there were no *eisteddfodau* in the 17th century, even though we have no account of any. From 1700 they surface again through the announcements in the 'Almanacs'. They were held at inns and were shoddy affairs. They had lost the support of the by now anglicized gentry, and the level of poetry was low.

The turning point came with Thomas Jones, of whose personal history little is known. He attended a typical *eisteddfod* of his time at Llangollen in January 1789 and determined to run a better one in Corwen the following May. He sought the backing of a London Welsh society, the Gwyneddigion. He publicized his *eisteddfod* widely and for the first time the general public was admitted. This was imitated over the following years in a number of places. There were at this time groups who were showing an interest in Welsh literature and musical societies were being formed: these were also organizing *eisteddfodau.*

In 1819 an *eisteddfod* was announced to take place in Carmarthen to commemorate that of 1450. It was initiated by a group of Welsh churchmen and the Dyfed 'Cambrian' Society. Both groups had done much to search out and publish ancient Welsh poets. This gathering, beginning on Thursday, July 8th 1819, was the beginning of the modern *Eisteddfod.* There were literary competitions and the winning poems and essays were read in public on the first day. On the second day there were competitions for harpists. It was strictly speaking after these two days of *Eisteddfod,* on the Saturday, that the two events happened which have become most significant since. In the evening the Bath Harmonic Society gave a concert. This, after two days of Welsh, was something of a sweetening of the pill to the anglicized gentry. Their support was essential, but their knowledge of Welsh was small and their interest in the finer points of the traditional Welsh poetic meters was less. On the morning of the same day Edward Williams (1747-1826, always known as 'Iolo Morganwg') held a 'Court of Bards' (Gorsedd y Beirdd).

Iolo Morganwg was one of Wales' most extraordinary characters. At a time when the Welsh Literary Parsons (Yr Hen Bersoniaid Llengar) as they came to be called, were editing and publishing the ancient poets, Iolo was inventing others and writing their 'works'. He built up an entirely fictional picture of ancient Glamorgan (his name 'Morganwg' means 'of Glamorgan'). He claimed that its bards had been angered by the changing of the old traditions at the Carmarthen *Eisteddfod* of 1450 and had alone preserved the old poetic meters in their purity. It was, of course, Iolo who had written the collection of 'ancient' poems which he claimed proved this. But his greatest invention was that of the 'Court of the Bards' (Gorsedd y Beirdd). From 1780 he lectured on the 'old' *Eisteddfodau* of Glamorgan:

then to this he added his fantasies about the Druids, the old Celtic priesthood, mentioned in Roman times, about whose religion and teaching next to nothing is known. He claimed that their traditions had been preserved, in Glamorgan of course, and that there were now only two men on whom the status of bard had been properly conferred by the Court, himself and one other. The London Welsh heard his 'revelations' in 1791 and held a *Gorsedd* on Primrose Hill in 1792.

This was the Iolo Morganwg who conducted his Court within a circle of small stones at Carmarthen in 1819, and gave the the somewhat surprised leaders of the *Eisteddfod* the ribbons of their bardic status. It took a long time for the connection between the *Gorsedd* and the *Eisteddfod* to be firmly established, in fact until the middle of the 19th century, but now no Royal National Eisteddfod is complete without the ceremonies in which the bards process in robes of white, blue and green, according to their status, and where the Archdruid presides. Most Welsh people now know that these 'ancient' ceremonies go back no farther than the beginning of the 19th century. But they do provide a needed element in the National Eisteddfod, and show that, for all his eccentricity (if not downright dishonesty), Iolo Morganwg had genius. He created something that the Welsh people have taken to their hearts. Now, based on his strange beginnings, the National Eisteddfod has a ceremonial that is non-military, and even anti-military, with its ceremonial cry "A oes heddwch?" (Is there peace?) to which the assembly replies "Heddwch". The whole has a non- establishment, non-conformist tone of voice, not the measured tones of the *Book of Common Prayer*. This is not surprising in that many of the Archdruids who have shaped these ceremonies have been chapel ministers.

To return to the *Eisteddfod* itself. The ideal of the men of 1819 was that there should be four regional societies, mounting each in turn their *eisteddfod,* under the supervision of a London Committee. This was attempted, but after a series from 1820-24 there was a pause. W.J.Rees wrote of a failure of support among the gentry, and added: "I am not sorry for the circumstances, as music is made too prominent a part of the proceedings", a sentiment that would surprise most supporters of the *Eisteddfod* today. He probably meant, however, that the performances of music were being put on for the benefit of the anglicized gentry and that they got in the way of the chief aim of the organizers, which was the promotion of the Welsh language and its literature. Some regional *eisteddfodau* were held, but the last of that particular series was in 1834. By this time however the *eisteddfod* movement was under way across the country, and hundreds of local and district *eisteddfodau* were being held. Since those early years of the 19th century the flow has since only been interrupted by war. It was in this period, in the second quarter of the 19th century, that musical competitions began to come into the programme, for singers, composers, and above all for the choirs which were springing up everywhere.

In 1858 came the first truly National Eisteddfod at Llangollen. It was in itself a strange affair but from it came a committee which, at the Denbigh Eisteddfod of 1860, decided to set the pattern that has been followed ever since of holding a great *Eisteddfod* once a year, alternately in North and South Wales. There was some disorder between 1868 and 1880 in which year a new Association was set up. Since then there has been a National Eisteddfod every year; the title 'Royal' was conferred in 1966.

The Royal National Eisteddfod takes place in August and lasts a week. It takes two years in each area to plan it and to raise the necessary funds. The list of competitions and the competition subjects and titles are published at each *Eisteddfod* for the next year. The *Eisteddfod* pavilion is erected on a large open site, and for the week the area around it is filled with stands occupied by the major Welsh societies, publishers and so on, together with the usual refreshment tents and banks. Many Societies hold their annual meetings during the *Eisteddfod* week, including the Hymn Society of Wales (Cymdeithas Emynau Cymraeg). The chief events are broadcast, the most intense coverage being given to the two ceremonies of Chairing and Crowning of the Bard for which the huge pavilion will be packed to the doors. There is considerable interest also in the Brass Band competitions, in those for the mixed and male-voice choirs and the various vocal solo competitions, culminating in the competition for the supreme vocal solo championship between the winners in the different sections. There are competitions for instrumental soloists, but despite efforts to build them up over the years they traditionally attract less interest than the others. The winning entries in the music composition classes once attracted a great deal of interest and tended to be set as competition pieces in the following years. With the growth of a music education of international standard in the university the winning pieces now tend to be in a contemporary style which very few of the *eisteddfod* performers would be able to master.

Every evening of the week is given over to a concert of some kind. There is usually a children's event. The Welsh National Youth Orchestra have in recent years given a fine account of themselves. The tradition has been that the choirs of the area in which the *Eisteddfod* takes place combine for some time in advance of the event in order to build up a large oratorio choir. They give concerts to raise funds for the *Eisteddfod* and then provide the backbone of the concerts during the week. This has now come under criticism. It is difficult with the dissolution of so many local choirs to gather enough good singers and the standard of the concerts has suffered accordingly just at a time when broadcasting and recording have provided the audience with a much higher standard by which the performances are judged. Such local societies as there are have been known to complain that the *Eisteddfod* has so disrupted their normal programme that it has taken several years to get back on their feet again afterwards.

Above all the National Eisteddfod is a place where the Welsh-speaking Welsh celebrate their Welshness. In the 19th century the language of the National Eisteddfod was often English. That has changed, and now there is a rule that only Welsh must be used on the *Eisteddfod* platform. This is understandable as a defence against the all-pervading English tongue, but taken to extremes it produces embarrassment, not the least to musicians who no longer wish to sing German Lieder, Italian arias or Latin masses in Welsh translations, whatever the fashion may have been in the past. Even worse is the resentment it causes in the majority of the population who no longer speak Welsh but feel insulted by any suggestion that they are not in some way properly Welsh, and excluded from an event that claims to be 'National'.

The *Eisteddfod* officially ends with the concert on Saturday evening. But the final use that is made of the Pavilion is in fact for the *Cymanfa Ganu* (The Singing Gathering) that takes place on the Sunday evening. This is now seen as an essential part of the programme and the Pavilion is packed to overflowing for an evening of hymn singing at which the old favourites are sung.

It is the National Eisteddfod that is known outside Wales, but there are even today hundreds, probably thousands of small *eisteddfodau* up and down the country, since societies, chapels, and schools all hold their competitive festivals. In many chapels Christmas Day was once a favourite date. There are many prestigious regional festivals which attract competition over a wide area and last several days. The Welsh-speaking youth movement *Urdd Gobaith Cymru* (The Welsh League of Youth) holds one annually at which the competition is very keen. These *eisteddfodau* were all once seen as the stepping stones to 'The National', but the pattern is not now so clear. This is in part because the standards at the National Eisteddfod are not very high in some sections. There are also problems too in persuading choirs, particularly the larger ones, to compete when the competition is in their usual holiday period and when they may have to travel long distances.

The International Eisteddfod held annually at Llangollen since 1947 is quite different from the genuine Welsh institution, though an inspired development from it. It is devoted mainly to folk-songs and dances and draws groups from all round the world to compete at a very high standard and to entertain each other and the public.

What effect does the *eisteddfod*, particularly the Royal National Eisteddfod, have on Welsh life? It is certainly a powerful influence in keeping alive the Welsh-speaking population's awareness of itself. A very large proportion of those who speak Welsh gather at 'the National' every year. It is a strong instrument in preserving the language together with the special Welsh-language culture. There is some danger however in doing this in the context of a competitive festival. There is always the danger of competition becoming an end in itself. There have, for example, been over the years choirs that have existed solely for the purpose of competing at *eisteddfodau*. This danger was seen and concern voiced in the 19th century when the movement was at its height. For the poet the winning of the crown or the chair is but a beginning, the signal that a new voice has arrived, one who is fully versed in his (or much less frequently her) craft. Once this has been signalled the public can expect to hear what he or she has to say as the gift is developed. In this way the *Eisteddfod* can work for the growth of the art of poetry in the community. The musical influence of the *Eisteddfod* is, however, largely conservative, with very few of the many young composers of Wales having their works performed on the Eisteddfod platform.

The *Eisteddfod* is simultaneously the despair and hope of sensitive Welsh men and women. It can be devisive, making it appear that the Welsh speakers claim to be the only true Welsh. Its standards can be very low: it can be quite out of touch with current trends and themes: its very methods and interests mean that it is always turning people's interests to the past: it can assume that if a thing is Welsh it is good, or that if it is the best available in Welsh it is good enough, despite international comparisons. On the other hand it continues to exist even though it requires vast labours: it attracts to its service Welsh men and women of outstanding gifts: despite this it touches not simply an elite but the whole of the Welsh speaking population within and beyond Wales: there have been times when it has been the instrument for moving the Welsh culture forward, and it could do this again. It may be like keeping a huge, sluggish dinosaur for a pet, but it remains obstinately alive and loved.

Chapter 3

CHRISTIANITY IN WALES

The Celtic Age

Looking at the map of Wales gives one picture of the Church there: the actual experience of traveling round Wales gives a different one.

The place names of Wales show how the Christian faith is written across the face of the land. To those who speak no Welsh this can be hidden. There are easily recognized places - Bethel and Bethlehem, Nasareth and Bethesda - named after chapels at a relatively late period. But all those names beginning with 'Llan-', some 500 of them, have a Christian origin. The word 'llan' signifies a Christian settlement, not a parish in the modern sense, though in later centuries parishes grew around them. The second part of the name is usually that of a saint. One of the fascinating things about the Welsh language is that the initial consonant under many circumstances is changed, 'mutated' is the technical term. The prefix 'Llan-' creates a 'soft mutation', so that adding 'Pedr' (Peter) produced 'Llanbedr' (St Peter's *llan* or community), and adding 'Mair' (Mary) 'Llanfair' (the 'f' is pronounced as 'v'), and adding 'Mihangel' (Michael the Archangel) 'Llanfihangel'. These Biblical names, however, come from the period when Roman influence predominated after the coming of the Normans. Before that was the age of the Celtic Church whose holy men spread Christianity over the land, often by settling in remote places and gathering followers who made a 'Llan'. The name of the founding saint might be given to the new *llan,* or the name of the founder's teacher or father-in-God. Thus there are many places called 'Llanddewi' ('Dewi' is the Welsh form of 'David' the patron saint of Wales): or 'Llandeilo' after St Teilo. But many of the names are unique, like 'Llandudno' (Tudno) or 'Llanrwst' (Grwst - the soft mutation makes the inital 'g' disappear). There are even Llanddeusant, Llandrisant and Llanpumsant (two, three and five saints). Even when the reference is not to a saint but to a local geographical feature (e.g. Llan-uwch-lyn means the *Llan* at the head of the lake) it is still an old Celtic site.

This is the Church on the map and on the signposts. But as you travel round Wales what you actually see as you pass through the towns and villages is rarely the old Parish Church which bears the saint's name. That is hidden behind the houses of the much later main street. At the cross-roads, or facing each other across the high street, are the chapels, with names on their gables like 'Seion', 'Moriah', 'Ebeneser', 'Horeb', 'Jerwsalem', 'Bethel': with dates such as 1820, 1860, 1905. Sometimes the name and date is all you will see. The chapels do not feel the need to publish times of services and the name of the minister. It is assumed that everyone in the village knows when the services are and who the minister is. There is a tremendous self-confidence in that. These are places that belong, that mean something in that community. All the more sad therefore to see that some have signs of neglect and disrepair: or to find a notice board, only to see that it announces that a small business undertaking has taken over the chapel. Better to see that perhaps than a gaping hole torn in the front and the capacious space of the old chapel open to the gaze of all as a garage and repair shop.

The Beginnings

We do not know how the Christian faith came to Wales. The light of history flickers in the most tantalizing way around what we should most dearly like to know. It is thought that there were two martyrs at Caerleon, Aaron and Julius. If so they probably perished at the beginning of the 4th century at the same time as the more famous St Alban in England, but in what persecution we do not know. Even before that, in the first half of the 3rd century, scholars in the Mediterranean - Tertullian in about 200 AD and Origen in about 240 AD - wrote implying that the existence of Christianity in Britain was well known. Across what is now the Welsh border, at the Roman villa of Corinium (now Cirencester), sometime during the 2nd or 3rd century a Christian was scratching on a red-plaster wall the words 'Pater Noster' (Our Father) in the shape of a cross. Christians were leaving their traces in other Roman villas in the 4th century - on walls and in the design of floor mosaics, on table-ware and signet rings, and although these villas were Roman we must not think of their inhabitants as Romans from Rome or even Italy. Many of them would have been Romanized Celts, ex-soldiers from Gaul and even from Britain itself.

By 397 Ninian was founding Candida Casa, his 'White Church' (we would call it his cathedral, tiny though it was) in Southern Galloway, beyond the northern boundaries of the Roman Empire. In South West England and in Wales and all up the western side of Britain there are Christian tombstones of the 5th to 7th centuries. These show that among the traders who used these western routes came Christians, ready to preach their faith in life and proud to rest beneath its symbol in death.

With the decline of the Empire in the 4th century and its eventual retreat from its most northerly outpost, there was a strong upsurge of the Celtic religion, and paganism certainly lingered on into the 6th century. But by the 5th century Christianity was established in the whole of Britain, most firmly of all in its Western parts. It did not come to its full flowering in Wales however until the 'Age of the Saints' in the 6th century.

This came with the spread of the monastic movement from its founding in the desert by Antony of Egypt. It was copied in Gaul, as there too Christians sought to rediscover some of the zeal and simplicity of life of the early Christians, and was given great impetus by the example of St Martin of Tours. Magnus Maximus, who had marched from Caernarvon to try to overthrow the Roman Emperor, became Martin's friend and after Maximus' defeat (383 AD) his queen Ellen and their sons Custennin (Constantine) and Peblig returned to Wales bringing this new inspiration with them. Llanbeblig (Peblig's Llan) is said to have been the first monastery in Wales, and all three, Ellen, Custennin and Peblig are remembered as saints. The same inspiration was moving into Wales from Ireland (and there was a very free flow of people and culture between all the Celtic Western parts of Britain at this time). The details of the lives of the Welsh saints are obscured by an overlay of folk-tale and miracle story in the 'Lives' written down many centuries later, but the main outlines can sometimes be discerned. The first flowering came in South Wales, with movement from the West often along the lines of the old Roman roads, which remained for centuries the only good means of communication in Wales.

The lives of the Welsh saints have a similar pattern whether they are great or small. They were often well-connected, the sons of princes and nobles, and they began as hermits, leaving all behind them in their search for a truly disciplined, godly life. Disciples gathered round them in their solitary places and formed a *clas* or monastery. This was not the kind of ordered community life which the Benedictines and their descendants fostered. These were essentially hermits living together. Each still had his own little beehive hut, though sometimes they were grouped around a larger hut in which they worshipped together. The whole would be surrounded by a fence (*bangor* - hence several Welsh place names). There was a contradiction in this kind of life of solitariness lived together. If the longing for a hermit's life was not satisfied by this the original founder would often move again to find another isolated place, or his followers would themselves move away, each founding another settlement (*llan*). Thus the names of some saints appear grouped in certain parts of the map of Wales, not because they themselves founded each *Llan* but because their disciples carried the name with them. The earliest names, Dyfrig, Illtud and Cadog are in the South, with the next generation, Dewi (David), Teilo and Padarn moving northward into central Wales. Finally in the north the great names are Deiniol, still revered in Bangor in Gwynedd of whose Cathedral he was the founder, with Cybi and Seiriol associated especially with Anglesey at the end of the century, and Beuno in the next century with his great foundation near Caernarvon.

In their search for loneliness and for stern surroundings for their ascetic life these saints sometimes made for the wild promontories of the coast and to islands. Thus, at the East and West extremes of Anglesey are Ynys Cybi (Cybi's Island: Caer-gybi is the Welsh for Holyhead, Cybi's stronghold) and Ynys Seiriol (Seiriol's Island, better known in English as Puffin Island). We may sometimes be deceived in this by reading into those times what is true of those places today. The great Cathedral which bears the name of St David is situated at the extreme end of the southern promontory of Cardigan Bay and is today remote. In St David's time Tŷ Ddewi (the Welsh name of the tiny 'city' means 'David's House') was a centre point of the trade and traffic that ran from Brittany to Celtic Cornwall (with its own Celtic language) and to Ireland and beyond. At the westernmost point of the northern promontory of Cardigan Bay there is however a truly remote place, Bardsey Island (Ynys Enlli, Enlli's Island) across a narrow but treacherous sound. Deiniol, Dyfrig and Padarn went there to die and it is said that 20,000 'saints' are buried there.

In all this talk of 'saints' it must be remembered that we are nearer the New Testament use of the word than our present one. Many of those who gave their names to the villages and towns of Wales were well schooled in their faith at the feet of some of the great Christians that have been mentioned. Some however were anything but gentle in their ways: most were what we would call quite ordinary Christians save in this, that they did move onwards and outwards and won the whole land for the Christian faith.

They carried the Celtic form of the faith. This same form was handed on to the Church in Ireland by the great age of the 6th century saints in Wales, bringing into being the golden age of the Church there. It became a great center of learning where civilization was kept alive while Europe was in the Dark Ages. A number of the great continental foundations of a later century were made from Ireland. The great illustrated manuscript, *The Book of Kells,* is the memorial to the learning, piety and art of Ireland in that period.

From Ireland the great Columba took the faith to Scotland in 563. He founded his monastery in Iona from which flowed a distinctive form of Christianity. Among Iona's ruins in this century has grown up a community from which in the 1950s and 60s a new inspiration flowed out to the whole of Scotland and beyond and which still exerts a creative influence.

The South East of England remained under the domination of its pagan Anglo-Saxon invaders, and it was to them that Augustine was sent from Rome by Pope Gregory in 596. The wife of King Ethelbert of Kent was already Christian and the king was soon himself converted and his people after him. Augustine is recorded by the Venerable Bede as having made two visits to meet the Welsh bishops to pursuade them to recognize him as the properly authorized archbishop, but to no avail. The first point of contention was probably that of authority. The Celtic Church did not feel the need to be tightly bound together under one head. (There was no Archbishop in Wales and, despite many attempts over the centuries to make one, that had to wait till the 20th century.) Thus the attempt to make the Celtic bishops recognize an outside authority was resisted. But there were also customs in which the Celtic Church had become conservative owing to its separation from the rest of Christendom. There was the matter of the shape of the tonsure, the shaven part of the head that was one sign of the monk. But above all they still kept Easter by the old calculation of the date while on the continent a new observance prevailed.

As the Roman mission pushed northwards the Columban Church was moving south: in 635 Aidan came from Iona to Lindsfarne and completed the conversion of Northumbria. Missionaries from Scotland and Ireland seem to have been active in many parts of England, while the Welsh part of the Celtic Church seemed to be resting after the glories of the Age of the Saints. In 664 the two missionary movements met to argue their differences at the Council of Whitby, presided over by Oswin, King of Northumbria. The representatives of the Celtic and the Roman sides argued their cases at great length before the King. The final decision may well have been made on political grounds, but publicly Oswin seized upon one point, that the Romans claimed, as heirs of St Peter, that they held the keys to heaven. For him this was decisive and he declared in favour of Rome. This was by no means the end of the struggle, but slowly the Celtic church gave way before the steady progress of Rome. Wales was left as the last isolated representative of the Celtic tradition. The Welsh clung for another century to their deep tradition of spirituality, but all the time they were being left behind, out of touch of the intellectual developments elsewhere and lacking the organizational skill which Rome brought. There is something spiritually powerful in a Church whose leadership is exercised by holy men on remote headlands and islands, who seek to live far from men and near to God. But when it is a matter of spiritual oversight and the organization of the necessary worldly aspects of the church then that body wins the day which places itself at the centres of communication, at the ports and great river crossings, as did the Roman mission.

Thus it was upon a church in decline in Wales that the Viking invaders fell during the 9th century, first as raiders and then to settle. The coastlands suffered most, where were the important monasteries. It became necessary to make alliance with Alfred of Wessex to defeat the common enemy. This broke at once both the political and the ecclesiastical isolation of Wales. Very gradually the Celtic ways gave place to Roman and the Welsh Church, consisting as it did of four independent bishoprics with no archbishop or central organization to make it a province of the church, turned to Canterbury for the consecration of its bishops. Full ecclesiastical domination from England followed the armies of Edward I (d.1301), and after a good deal of unrest the Welsh dioceses came to be part of the province of Canterbury, for good and ill. The Welsh church was poor and few of those appointed Bishops there could speak the language or understand the problems that their clergy faced. There were those that encouraged the provision of devotional material in Welsh, so that even before the

Reformation there were parts of the Bible available in Welsh, and behind the troubles and often scandals of the Bishops there was a quiet ministry by priests, some well educated, but most scarcely more educated than their flock.

The Reformation

The Protestant Reformation under Henry VIII and his successors was a distant matter to the Welsh. The monasteries in Wales were disolved as elsewhere. The gentry, dependent on the crown as they were, took their lead from England in matters of religion as in other things. With the Welsh Tudors on the throne many Welshmen had made their way in the court, in public service and in the law, but the price was that they became anglicized in dress and manners and above all in language, and they carried this influence back into Wales. The Bishops were of this same class and they, for the most part, payed less attention to their Welsh dioceses than to furthering their careers in church and state (in the hope of moving to an English diocese) and to the cares of other church offices which they held in plurality in England.

In 1563 a law was passed ordering the four Welsh Bishops together with the Bishop of Hereford to prepare a translation of the Bible and *The Book of Common Prayer* by March 1st (St David's Day) 1566, a move that was as much political as an attempt to provide for the spiritual needs of the Welsh. It appears that Richard Davies (?1501-81), Bishop of St David's, translated *The Book of Common Prayer* himself, and that he recruited William Salesbury (?1520-?84) for the work on the Bible, together with Thomas Huet (d.1591). *The Book of Common Prayer* and the New Testament came out in 1567. The choice of Salesbury was a wise one in that he set a fine standard of style. It was unfortunate that he had a strange theory of spelling which made his work difficult to read. Thus a revision of the New Testament as well as a translation of the Old Testament were needed and both were provided in 1588 with the help of others by William Morgan (?1541-1604), who later became Bishop of Llandaf and then of St Asaph. He set a high standard, using a slightly archaic Welsh, that of the traditional poets, and subsequent revisions polished his version and heightened yet more the nobility of the style. Though attempts at modern translations were made in the earlier years of the 20th century it was not until the 1970s that a new version of the New

Testament began in any way to replace it. Thus the influence of William Morgan's Bible on the Welsh language and the Welsh mode of thought has lasted for a full four centuries and has been beyond calculation in its depth and importance.

After the Reformation

The religious controversies that followed the Reformation remained distant matters to the Welsh, many of whom remained faithful to their old Roman Catholic ways of worship. But Puritanism did have its effect in the foundation of the Old Dissenters. Thus on the eve of the great Revival of the 18th century which has shaped all the subsequent history of Wales there were in 1715 perhaps some 3,000 Quakers; about 20 Baptist congregations, and some 80 congregations of Presbyterians and Congregationalists. At the heart of their faith was essentially the need and right of the individual to his own judgment, and thus his right to join, by agreement, with those like-minded in an independent congregation. Though this sounds quite innocent and right today it was, in those days, a deeply devisive matter and smacked of rebellion against the authority of the Crown.

The Old Dissent appealed to all classes but their strength lay chiefly in the minor gentry and with the business men, since many of these congregations are to be found in the lowland and border areas where ideas flowed along with trade. They must not be confused with the kind of revival that was to come. Their appeal was to the mind not to the emotions: all life was to be lived in the light of faith, and so the conscience must be educated and this led to a general emphasis on education and the publication of devotional and theological books, mainly translations from English. Their 'dissenting academies' were a powerful educational influence, often providing a more broadly based education than Oxford or Cambridge were able to give at that time. Their worship was sober and careful. They sang metrical psalms (by many accounts very badly) with hymns coming into their worship by the early 18th century: the sermon was long and weighty. They often met in houses and barns, and their meeting houses when they built them were simple and unadorned but not necessarily ugly. They gathered for worship once on Sunday, the rest of the day being set aside for worship at home and 'catechizing', that is the instruction of children and servants. By the early years of the 18th century many of them realized that something was lacking: the fire had dwindled, and their urging and preaching and praying became part of the foundation of the Revival, from which in turn they were to receive new life.

The Established Church was in a poor condition. Its form of government remained mediaeval in a changed world. What was needed was a revision of parish boundaries, a reform in finances and the building of new churches. Such changes were impossible because those in power were the ones who benefited from the corrupt condition of the time. Bishops, with a few honourable exceptions, remained absentees: the old office of archdeacon, who had represented the Bishop in the day to day running of the diocese, had declined. The Bishop was supposed to 'visit' his diocese, that is to tour and to ask for written returns on the state of the parishes: few did this more than once in their episcopate, and since mass confirmations went with the visitation few were confirmed (though the rules of the church did not bar the unconfirmed from communion). Clergy who were well connected held many appointments simultaneously and received their incomes. This meant that curates had to be engaged to take the services. They were all too often ill-paid and therefore themselves had to hold a number of curacies to be able to live. Thus in the parish church the one service on a Sunday was often hurried through in time for the clergyman to rush off to another parish to take yet another service; there was little preaching; the sacrament was celebrated at best monthly and on the festivals; the teaching of the catechism was neglected. However, the feast day of the saint in whose name the local parish church was dedicated was celebrated with enthusiasm. This could be a rowdy occasion with games and singing and dancing, and the leaders of the Revival were later to condemn these 'patronal festivals' in most severe terms. They did however give the parishioners a welcome holiday and showed the extent to which the life of the Church was woven into the life of the people. Largely, however, the Established Church had lost their love and admiration. The Church belonged, it was felt, to the anglicized gentry. In the churches this was made all too clear week by week by the way the churchwardens allotted seats at the services by class and wealth.

The clergy were not, however, ill-educated and attempts were made to provide education for the people. Religious societies flourished. Especially important after its founding in 1698 was the

Society for Promoting Christian Knowledge (S.P.C.K.) which had much support in Wales and published most of the Welsh prose that came out in the next forty years. Charity schools were founded by churchmen and dissenters, but few survived more than a short life; what was done served to heighten a longing that the Revival was left to fill.

The most notable piece of work was by a clergyman of the Established Church, Gruffydd Jones (1683-1761), a man who in many ways was a bridge from the old to the new in Wales. He attended Queen Elizabeth School, Carmarthen but did not go on from there to university. From the time of his ordination as deacon in 1708 he was on the lists of S.P.C.K. as a teacher. But his chief aim in life always was to save souls and his tremendous work to further education in Wales was undertaken in order that every-one should be able to read the Bible. His ambition was to see a copy in every home. So he corresponded endlessly with S.P.C.K. to get a new edition of the Welsh Bible published and to have the New Testament available in large print. He was often out of favour with his bishop because he preached outside the church building and often in churches in other parishes without the permission of the incumbent, gathering many hundreds to hear him wherever he went (and this, remember, a quarter of a century before the Revival). He travelled through England and Scotland, possibly preaching before Queen Anne. In 1716 he was appointed Rector of Llanddowror, Carmarthenshire, where he remained for the rest of his life. In 1731 he began the work for which he is best remembered, his circulating schools. In creating these, a teacher (who had to be sober, godly, a member of the Church of England and patriotic), was invited, preferably by the vicar of the parish, to set up a school: there the children during the day and adults in the evening were taught simply to read; they were not even taught to write. When a sufficient standard was reached, usually after some six months, the teacher moved on to set up another school. Many of the early Methodist leaders began as circulating teachers and mingled their preaching and exhorting with their work. They turned to Gruffydd Jones for counsel; he gave it freely and worked with them at first. As the Revival spread, however, it is clear that Gruffydd Jones was in a difficult position. Many who supported his schools and particularly S.P.C.K. were hostile to the Methodists. For some years he managed to keep the two sides of his work separate (perhaps the language difference helped), but in the end he hardened towards the Methodists and, probably to defend his schools, dissociated himself from the movement. Diplomatically he may well have read the needs of the time correctly, for the S.P.C.K. continued to support the circulating schools long after his death.

Thus by 1730 Wales was a land prepared for Revival: there was a widespread thirst for a living faith: there were many who read their Bibles but needed to hear its meaning: there were those who worked and prayed for a new spirit in the Church. Yet none of the seed that was sown had more than a feeble growth until 1735.

The Great Awakening

On Palm Sunday 1735 a young schoolmaster, Howel Harris (1714-73), from Trefeca-fach (Trevecca) in Breconshire, attended service in his parish church of Talgarth. He heard the Vicar, Pryce Davies, exhorting his people to come to Communion on Easter Day, despite any feeling of unworthiness they might have: "You say you are not fit to come to the Table. Well then, I say that you are not fit to pray: yes, you are not fit to live, nor fit, either, to die". Harris was touched, and received Communion for the first time that Easter, and again, unprepared, the following Sunday. Then he began to read devotional books, and learned that he could be forgiven his sins in receiving Communion in faith. He went to Communion again on Whit Sunday, and returned, full of love and joy that his sins were forgiven.

On that first Palm Sunday, he had already moved one other person to repentance by repeating Vicar Davies' call. Now he used every opportunity to read the Bible and devotional books to neighbours, and to exhort and encourage wherever he went. By August he had formed a rudimentary Society of those 'who are willing to join me in a Strict Observation of our Duty': they bound themselves to attend the worship of their parish church Sunday by Sunday and to receive the sacrament monthly. The very heart of the Revival and the chief means of securing its ground are to be found in these activities, in the earnest preaching and counselling (or exhorting), in the small society meeting for mutual support in the living of a Christian life, all bound together by attendance at the Parish Church especially for the Sacrament. All this was three years before the conversion experience of the Wesleys. Harris, like the Wesleys, remained loyal to the Established Church despite early contacts with sympathetic Baptists and others and almost continuous opposition from the Church authorities. In May 1736 he went to take counsel with Gruffydd Jones, preaching as he went. That same year he applied to his bishop for ordination, but was denied then and later. This was to prove a grave weakness both to Harris and in the movement, for Harris was always aware of his lack of status when working alongside those who had been ordained.

Others who had been moved by him began to exhort and counsel (*cynghori* is the Welsh word: it means 'to counsel' but its equivalent in English documents of the time is 'exhort'). Some clergy joined the movement, as did some dissenting ministers. The movement spread, chiefly at first across South Wales, where the Church had been most neglectful and where the spiritual hunger was greatest. Harris gradually found support among local gentry, an important factor in protecting him from enemies. These included John Williams of Ynys-grin, whose daughter Anne he married in 1744, and Marmaduke Gwynne of Garth near Llangamarch (whose daughter Sally married Charles Wesley in 1749). He found a close friend in Howel Davies (1716-70), who came to Talgarth as a schoolmaster in 1737, was converted and came to live with his 'father-in-God'. Davies was ordained priest in 1740 and is celebrated in Welsh Methodist history as 'the Apostle of Pembrokeshire' though his importance in the movement was far wider than that name implies.

Daniel Rowland

The other truly great name in the history of the Revival is that of Daniel Rowland. Harris may well have been the founder of the movement, but it is clear that, for Welsh Methodists, Rowland is the great Apostle and Preacher. Harris left a mountain of documents behind him in the form of diaries, letters and controversial writings. Rowland's papers seem to have been passed to Lady Huntingdon with a view to the writing of a biography, and then lost. For this reason we know much less about him and much that we do know comes from Harris. He was probably born in 1711 in Nantgwnlle in Cardiganshire where his father had charge of that parish together with the neighbouring Llangeitho. It is clear that he received a good education, though he did not go to university. His father died in 1731 and his brother John took over the parish of Llangeitho. It appears that Daniel must have spent some time about then with Gruffydd Jones. He was ordained deacon in 1734 by the Bishop of St David's, having walked to London for the purpose. He at first served as assistant curate to his brother. In 1735 he was ordained priest, and possibly again visited Gruffydd Jones. The stories that he was at this time something of a drunkard and slack in his ministry are unlikely to be true. They probably refer to no more than his taking part in the ordinary social events of the parish, including those of the church's own patronal festival. What is certainly true is that he was lively with a strong sense of humour.

It appears that he first began to draw large congregations by his powerful preaching of the dangers of sin and the need to flee from the wrath to come. It may well have been through the ministry of Gruffydd Jones that he learnt the reality of forgiveness won on the Cross. It is probable that in 1736 he was preaching beyond the bounds of his own parish. Thus in two areas of South Wales the Revival began independently, the only link being that both leaders went to Gruffydd Jones for counsel.

In 1737 Harris heard Rowland preach and he reports that his heart went out to him in love. He visited Llangeitho later in the year but it was impossible for the two men to have frequent meetings to plan the movement. One reason for this was that travel in Wales was at that time very slow. Of necessity therefore the movement went forward in a somewhat disconnected fashion. The leaders in each part of Wales took the opportunities that were open to them in their area. Each one was thankful to hear of the others from time to time and to know that through one means or another the cause prospered.

Growth and Division

Howel Harris cannot have been aware that some words he spoke at Talgarth in 1737 (or possibly in 1738) were going to have a momentous effect on the history of Christianity in Wales. Among those who heard him was a young student, William Williams from Carmarthenshire. He had come in 1737 to the Dissenting Academy at Chancefield, not half a mile from Talgarth, run by the redoubtable scholar Vavasor Griffith, with the purpose of studying to be a doctor. He lived with his uncle in the village of Talgarth, and on his way back there from

Chancefield (this is the most likely reconstruction by Gomer Roberts of this heavily romanticized story) he heard Howel Harris preach in the churchyard after a service in the church. His heart was touched and he yielded himself to the call of Christ. He completed his education, but, now under the influence of Howel Harris and not the dissenters. On Harris' advice he was ordained in 1740 to be curate of Llanwrtyd. (See page 93 for a fuller account of William Williams.)

By now the Spirit was moving in England. In December 1738 George Whitfield wrote to Harris in the warmest terms. Harris replied giving an account of how things stood in Wales. The two met in Cardiff in February 1739 and we have warm accounts from each of them of the meeting. At this meeting Whitfield learnt an important lesson, that open-air preaching was a most effective way of spreading the gospel. As a priest of the Established Church he had never dreamed of doing such a thing: nor had John Wesley. Now they both followed Harris' example (learnt in all probability from Gruffydd Jones). The results astonished them, and this became an important means of spreading the Revival in England too. Harris met John Wesley in June 1739 and again there was much warmth in the encounter.

Harris did not himself venture into North Wales at this time. Daniel Rowland however did and William Williams after him. Soon, despite some harsh treatment and harsher words, the re- vival spread there too. By 1742, the movement had been planted in small gatherings all over Wales. To Harris fell the task of organizing the movement by means of forming Societies. This was not a new idea. It had been attempted some fifty years before and an influential book had been written by Dr Woodward, *An Account of the Religious Societies in the City of London etc* (1697). It was several times reprinted and 'Abstracts' from it were published by S.P.C.K. It seems that Rowland also was forming societies, but Harris was the indefatigable visitor and organizer, wearing himself out physically in travel, sitting up late exhorting and counselling and rising early to journey on foot to the next society. The roads at this time in Wales were appalling and the Revival spread mainly along the drovers' tracks. Only toward the end of the century did the Turnpike Trusts begin to build a network of toll-roads that were to speed communication.

In all this activity and the evident work of the Spirit in touching men and women's hearts in all classes of society there were also signs of disagreement. In England, Wesley and Whitfield split over doctrinal matters in 1741. In Wales too there was growing unease. This was not however on doctrinal grounds, for the revival in Wales was always predominantly Calvinistic in outlook. While there was nothing specifically Welsh in the message there seems to have been an affinity in the Welsh spirit for this severe, authoritarian view of Christianity. The faith of the Welsh hinterland had been little affected by the Reformation. Many were still Roman Catholic at heart, looking still for a clear presentation of what they were to believe and for a firm discipline. The Puritans with their emphasis on the intellect and on the individual conscience made little impact except on the borders. What the true native Welsh man and woman needed, it seemed, was to be given a word directed to the heart more than to the head. Harris himself put it thus in 1747:

> We preach chiefly to the heart and the spirit . . .
> faith in the heart rather than enlightenment in the
> head. We awake the soul to its depths by carrying
> the conviction to its very roots . . . . they leave the
> soul quiet and unawakened . . . They do not search
> the heart.

This was the appeal of the Welsh Revival and there was little doctrinal controversy concerning its main thrust. High Calvinism did not reach the movement till the 19th century. The Calvinism of the 18th century Revival in Wales spoke of all mankind being encompassed in sin, of the worthlessness of 'works', of the coming judgment and of salvation in Christ alone for those who are his elect. This, with the discipline that went with it, was what was preached in Wales and in the end set the temper of thought of the nation.

The division in Wales centred on the difference in personality of the two leaders, Harris and Rowland. From Harris' massive diaries it is possible to gain a clear picture of the intensity of his nature, his continual searching of his soul concerning himself and his reactions to others. It is clear that he often saw the other leaders, especially Rowland, as frivolous: what cause was there to laugh when there was so much work to be undertaken, and work of such great importance as the saving of souls - one's own and others'? Besides this, Harris was a layman and the lay exhorters whom he placed at the head of his new societies resented the restrictions he placed on their movements and activities, seeing the freedom he allowed himself. Harris was not one to accept the others as leaders of the movement and so he looked outside Wales and invited Whitfield to head a General Session at Watford near Caerphilly.

Since their first encounter a friendship had grown up between Whitfield and Harris and from 1739 Harris regularly visited London. This was yet another point of disagreement with Rowland who saw the need for Harris' presence in Wales. Harris met the Wesleys in London and often preached in Whitfield's Tabernacle. In 1741 he was in London for 3 months trying in vain to heal the breach between the Wesleys and Whitfield. In 1743 it was Whitfield's turn to come to Wales 'to fill a vacuum which neither of those imperious men, Harris and Rowland, would allow the other to fill'. It was to be the first official meeting of the Calvinistic section of the Revival in both England and Wales.

The natural outcome of the meeting was that Whitfield was acknowledged as head of the movement, with Harris as his Deputy and general overseer of Welsh Methodism, an office for which his organizational genius fitted him well. In 1744 Whitfield went to America, leaving Harris in charge of the London Tabernacle, and, although a layman, the head of the Calvinistic movement in England and Wales. It must be accounted a weakness in him and was certainly a weakness in the movement that he was determined to have and to keep his supremacy: there were those who called him "Pope". Rowland was equally determined not to be ruled by Harris, an ordained minister by a layman. The gap between them widened. Doctrinal differences did arise, especially when Harris, whose power was as a preacher and organizer, not as a theologian, tackled difficult matters such as the doctrine of the Person of Christ. He took over from his Moravian friends their emphasis on the Blood of Christ, speaking even of 'The Blood of God'. Rowland's wise counsel on the dangers of such expressions could by now only confirm Harris in his way of thought, such was the hostility between them. By 1746 there was outright opposition between the two. This became public in a Conference in Trevecca in June, when it would seem that all the preachers and exhorters alike set upon Harris for his teaching and his high handed attitude. Rowland was magnificent in the pulpit, as even Harris allowed, but could be as spiteful and bitter-tongued as Harris out of it. In October a similar Conference had before it a well-prepared resolution to remove Harris from office and to put Rowland in his place, with power to direct preachers and exhorters. Harris declared himself willing to go, but not willing to put himself under Rowland's authority. His supporters rallied around him and he was re-appointed, but there could be no real return to the position of 1739. 1747 was a quiet year, largely because Harris spent over half of it in England, though questions of authority and discipline did arise. On Whitfield's return in 1748 Harris was again able to turn his attention to Wales where his gifts as organizer were sadly missed. By March 1749 Harris was even preaching on Rowland's home ground in Llangeitho with something of the old love between the two leaders. But this was to be the last period of peace for some years.

Harris had never been fortunate in his choice of intimate friends, who were, in his own word, his 'eyes' on what was going on in the movement. His choice now was disastrous. On a preaching tour in Caernarvonshire in October 1748 Harris met Madam Sidney Griffith, a married woman, separated from her husband, who had recently been converted. Early in 1749 she visited Llangeitho, as did so many others wishing to hear Rowland preach, and in February accompanied Rowland to the Conference in Errwd where she again met Harris and went on to stay three days in Trevecca. In July Harris was again in North Wales and met her with her maid, discoursed with her, and invited her to travel with him to the Conference in Llangeitho. On the journey a kind of spiritual friendship developed at a most ecstatic level (at least on Harris' side) and he finds when he is in London in August that he is experiencing 'a total change . . . a new life'. On his return in September, Madam Griffith is waiting for him in Trevecca, expelled from her home by her husband. The comings and goings are manifold: rumour is rife. Howell and Ann Harris arrive in London having met Madam Griffith and her son on the road, and Harris is surprised that Whitfield does not invite him to preach! Harris, still convinced that she is 'an unerring expounder of the will of God', nevertheless remarks on her high spending and lack of charity. On his return to Wales in February 1750 he resisted his friends' advice in favour of hers and took her about with him 'like some ark of the covenant', to quote his opponents, but to him 'a prophetess', 'Debora to his Barac', while his enemies made other scriptural references, particularly to Samson and Delilah. The reference was sadly apt. It is clear that his feelings for her were not returned with anything like warmth, at least to judge by her letters. For many in the movement Harris' lack of wisdom in his relationship with Madam Griffith made a final rift inevitable.

In May a Conference was held in Central Wales at Llanidloes. It is known as the Conference of the Division, but the formal split did not take place there, though it was seen as inevitable. There were the accusations and counter-accusations, by now all too familiar, and the two parties left the meeting to group themselves as 'Rowland's People' and 'Harris' People'. As ever his own worst enemy, Harris lost some of his own wisest friends among his own People by refusing to listen to their good advice. Rowland's People included William Williams Pantycelyn and Howell Davies. In a final chance meeting between Harris, Rowland and Williams, Harris asked whether they accepted the common accusation that his association with Madam Griffith was adulterous. They did not. At least that amount of trust remained between former workers together for the Lord.

Between 1750 and 1752 Harris called together a number of Conferences, and later, meetings he called Councils. But he could see that he was losing support and began to make gestures that signified that he saw Rowland's People as the continuing Methodist Revival in Wales. By 1752 he had retreated to Trevecca. He was only 36, though he had complained some years before of looking and feeling prematurely aged, as well he might with all his incessant labours, travelling, preaching and exhorting. His own unyielding and even intransigent spirit had driven him on where others rested, took refreshment and found entertainment (his constant complaint against Rowland). In need of rest he may have been. Finished, by no means, for it was during the years of division that he accomplished perhaps his most unique work.

Trevecca

Howel Harris had as early as 1736 resolved 'to build an Alms House and a School'. He admired similar work elsewhere, and he admired the community life of the Moravians. So he began to give flesh and bone to his dream in Trevecca. In April 1752 he pulled down the old house: part was rebuilt, ready for its new purpose, by July, and there were rooms ready by the winter. The work went on inside and out for 20 years, and always Harris was in charge, making every decision large and small with prayer. A Chapel was opened in 1758 with a sermon by Harris on Christmas Day. Between 1769 and 1772 the building was enlarged for Lady Huntingdon.

Harris was in debt when he began building, but he received generous gifts and loans. Most important of all, people began to arrive and became the Trevecca Family. By 1755 there were 100 in Trevecca itself and 50 in farms round about, some of them bought or rented for the purpose. Harris ruled everything with great strictness. His intention had been that Madam Griffith should rule the women, but she died in May 1752. His wife Ann was not suited to the work. A series of ladies were appointed to be over the women and make a stormy passage through Harris' diaries. Finally Hanna Bowen took over in 1755, remaining, with some interruptions, for 15 years, looking after the house, taking care of the women and teaching the children.

In the light of what has been said about the spiritual needs of the Welsh not having been met between the time of the Mediaeval Roman Church and the Methodist Revival, it is interesting to note that Harris' community was much nearer in spirit to the Benedictine or Cistercian monastery than to the Celtic. All members of the community, for example, had to work. There were a great number of crafts represented: the Trevecca carpenters were well respected and the cloth made at Trevecca sold far and wide. One of the most important of the crafts was printing for which Harris sent James Pritchard to London to learn the trade. There was tight control over the Family's personal lives, over marriage in particular, and a constant personal counselling on the state of each member's soul was Harris' particular ministry. These were ordinary people. They were under no vow; they came and they went, and one suspects that they often went because of Harris' firm discipline. But they came because of his preaching and counselling, and that was what they received in generous measure, from his bed in the early years when he was in poor health, then in the new Chapel. They welcomed many visitors, the great names of the Revival in England among them. Lady Huntingdon built a college for her preachers facing the main house, in which she had been provided with her own rooms.

It was inevitable that such a personal vision should not long outlive the founder, and those who had been with him. Harris died in 1773 and the Family came to an end officially in 1839. But even now Trevecca remains an important Christian centre of education. It has its own atmosphere and is important in the Christian heart and affection of Wales.

The Healing

The time of division was one in which even if the work did not stop it certainly slackened in pace. Without Harris it was wanting in the discipline that turns initial enthusiasm into true spiritual growth. The old hurts were however beginning to heal and by 1756 there were friendly overtures being made and some of 'Rowlands People' visited Harris from time to time. By 1759 a meeting between the leaders was possible at which reconciliation was attempted, but many still feared that Harris would try to take command again and rule in too authoritarian a style.

This was a time, however, when there was fear of invasion by France, and this was seen by Harris, as by many others, as a challenge to a kind of holy war in defence of Protestantism against the Papacy. Harris received a commission as an Ensign and raised a platoon of militia (he who had seemed at the point of death at the time of the division). Thus, for the next 2 years he was away on military duty in England. By May 1762 Rowland was writing a letter signed by himself and the leading spirits of his 'People', anticipating Harris' return to Trevecca, and inviting him to return at the same time to the work. This he did when he resigned his commission at the end of the year.

Meanwhile, as a kind of sign and seal upon the healing of the division, a new Revival had broken out. It was not this time the quiet working of the leaven in widely separated places as at first, but a movement that swept across the land, with great gatherings of people singing the new hymns, especially William Williams' new collection *The Songs of those upon the Sea of Glass*. That book seemed able to produce a revival wherever it was introduced.

A meeting of the renewed Association was held in Trevecca itself in May 1763 and the ground rules again asserted that this was no new sect, but that all were to be members of the Church of England and to receive communion in the Parish Church.

The new Revival continued in strength for 2 or 3 years. Those unsympathetic to it complained of the new activity of the Methodists "singing, capering, bawling, fainting, thumping, and a variety of other exercises". In the years that followed, chapels were being built up and down the country, and from 1778 it became necessary to raise a 'Halfpenny Collection', a weekly contribution from each member to assist in this development.

During these years Llangeitho, always important as the place where Rowland preached, increased as a second focus of the Revival alongside Trevecca. People came to live at Trevecca. They made pilgrimages to Llangeitho, above all for the 'last Sunday in the Month' for communion. On that Sunday there was no service in the villages around and people made pilgrimages from far and wide, as often as once every two or three months, riding, on foot, by sea. On Saturday they joined in the services. At 11 a.m. Rowland would preach: later in the day there was a service of preparation, and on Sunday 1,200 to 1,500 people would receive communion, two or three other priests assisting Daniel Rowland in the administration. Those who travelled from far would be given accommodation and food on the local farms and even in the big houses, sleeping by the score on straw in the barns. Then on the Monday they would set off home, singing and praying on the way, often having to endure mockery and even violence from those still hostile to the Revival.

Thus was the Revival strengthened and established by two institutions unique to the movement in Wales. Each in their turn reflected the character of the man at its centre: Llangeitho with its great congregations gathering around Rowland, the great preacher: Trevecca with its community gathered around Harris, the great counsellor and organizer. A third force assisted the other two, the hymns, above all the hymns of the third great leader, William Williams.

Howell Davies died in 1770. Harris died in 1773, old and worn out by the age of 51. Rowland lived to be 67 (or 69 - there is some mystery about the date of his birth). He died on the 16th of October 1790. It was a Saturday and many were present in Llangeitho expecting him once again to come and lead them in preparation for communion. The meeting had begun when news came of his death, and the congregation broke up and made its way home in mourning. William Williams died in 1791, and of the four it is his voice that lives on, and will live on even if, as seems inevitable, the mark that these founding fathers of Methodism left on the nation gradually fades.

Consolidation and Education

The first leaders left no clear successor, but the movement continued to grow in strength. There was much building of chapels. To judge from the reports of travellers in Wales at the turn of the century there was no lessening of fervour in the Methodists' worship. These English visitors complain of the shouting of the preachers, the tempestuous hymn singing and the 'jumping', men and especially women leaping, hands up-raised, praising God.

A new leader eventually emerged in the person of Thomas Charles of Bala in North Wales (1755-1814). Although he was only 6 when Gruffydd Jones, Llanddowror died, Thomas Charles can be counted in many ways his spiritual descendant: indeed he received his first education in the school at Llanddowror before moving to the Carmarthen Dissenting Academy. He travelled from there to hear Daniel Rowland preach and by his own testimony was converted in January 1773. After graduating at Jesus College, Oxford he was ordained and served 3 years in England. In 1783 he moved to North Wales, to take up an assistant curacy in Merionethshire and to marry Sally Jones of Bala, which was a prosperous market town and by then a considerable centre of Methodism. He was ejected from his parish 3 months after his marriage because of his friendship towards the Methodists and never held another appointment in the established church, being able to rely on the success of the business run by his wife. He increasingly identified himself with the Methodist Society in Bala and was active in Methodism at large. He became desperately concerned by the lack of education he found everywhere, seeing that even preaching was weakened if the congregation could not respond to the preacher's Biblical references. He opened a school at the Methodist meeting house in Bala for the children of the Society and thus began his life's work. At first he rejected the Sunday School, already a force in England, in favour of circulating schools on the model of Gruffydd Jones. His was a smaller movement than the earlier one, but much more closely organized, catering for adults as well as children. He personally produced teaching material and inspected the work. As with Grufydd Jones his principal aim was always the salvation of souls.

Others were starting Sunday Schools on English models and only reluctantly did Thomas Charles move to support them, 1797 being a turning point after the best part of a year in London when he must have studied the movement with some care. He now put all his energy behind the organizing of Sunday and weeknight schools, and the Welsh Sunday School Movement had truly begun.

It was different from the movement in England and remains so. The Welsh Sunday School is more democratic than the English, being controlled by the teachers who are chosen from among the members. It is open to both sexes of all ages. The learning process is seen as life long, and discussion became the most important method of learning.

Many aspects of Welsh national life were to grow from the Sunday School. Here the 'non-conformist conscience' was developed, together with a feeling for democracy and self-expression. Here too a love of singing was fostered, especially when in the second half of the 19th century Tonic-sol-fa was introduced and taught in the Sunday Schools. They believed in the principle that no Christian is properly educated who cannot sing his or her part in the Church's song. When in the 19th century the migration to the industrial areas began, the Sunday Schools were taken there too and proved a cohesive element in societies whose members had been uprooted and thrust into a new and harsh world.

Testimony abounds to the respect accorded to the movement in the years of its strength. In 1847 the Education Commissioners found Sunday Schools superior to any other provider of education at the time. Their weakness was that, though they were intended to feed the Church with members, the Sunday School tended to draw away from the Church and became a separate entity, a church within a church in all the denominations.

Ascendancy and Decline

Up to this point the Methodist Revival had remained within the Established Church of England, being officially a movement of renewal within it, as the founders insisted. With their deaths it was left to Thomas Charles to shepherd the movement to face the reality of their existence as a separate body. It was a task he undertook unwillingly. By the 1790s a number of groups of Methodists had felt obliged to register under the law as dissenting chapels. Methodists would not turn to what they saw as the godless clergy of the parish churches for baptism and communion: the episcopally ordained clergy in the movement had always been few in the South and even fewer in the North and now the calls on them were far too great. Over the early years of the new century leaders and members alike agonized over the problem and took a many years to reach a decision. The result was that when in 1811 lay preachers were set asided to administer the Sacraments the move was met with sober relief. 'The Calvinistic Methodists' were now one more dissenting body alongside the old dissent. They did not form any kind of cohesive body with them. There was indeed considerable hostility. Baptists complained that Methodism with its fervour was invading their ranks. By 1800 the Wesleyan Methodists with their Arminian doctrines had begun to move into Wales. Their success came only in certain areas, and they were generally suspected by all the older groups of Welsh origin. To this day in Welsh it is necessary to distinguish carefully between the 'Methodists', that is the Calvinists, and the 'Wesleyans'.

It is not necessary for a general understanding of the history of the church in this period to go into detail over the doctrinal controversies which racked the Methodists and the other denominations in the early years of the nineteenth century. The important point is that during these years the hold of the chapels over the population became so complete that Welsh culture as we know it came into being. This was true not only of the Calvinistic Methodists ('The Old Body' - *Yr Hen Gorff* - as it came to be known) the largest single denomination, but of the other chapels, Congregationalist, Baptist and Wesleyans. At the religious census of 1851 over 80% of those who worshipped on the census Sunday had done so in a nonconformist chapel, though to give a complete picture it has to be noted that 50% of the adult population worshipped nowhere. Not even in Wales was there ever a time when everyone went to church or chapel on Sunday!

Great changes were taking place in Wales with great shifts of population into the industrial areas of South Wales where new villages and towns began to grow up around the mines, the blast furnaces and the steel rolling mills. Though the migration to America was at this time very considerable, the internal migration was even greater. The new industries were being manned by Welshmen, moving from impoverished country areas. Their chapels came with them. Though every place was theoretically within a Church of England parish and under the care of its clergy, the parish churches were at the centres of the old, pre-industrial communities and not where the population was growing. The organization of the established church was not designed to meet such changes and because of that was painfully slow in providing for the new needs. The chapels could move in more quickly and did so, providing centres of Welsh culture and at least some education in their Sunday Schools. They gave too that element of hope and meaning to life in the appalling conditions of the here and now, and a hope of a better life hereafter. It is no wonder that so many of the hymns sing so powerfully of heaven.

The ebb and flow of religious life in Wales is difficult to follow in detail but the general picture is tolerably clear. The Established Church was becoming acutely conscious that it was no longer the church of the bulk of the population. Calls were being heard by mid-century for its disestablishment, but the church leaders were in no mood to acquiesce in so revolutionary a step. The Church of England was in fact fighting back. It had by 1820 created the first educational establishment in Wales of a university standard in St David's College, Lampeter (Llanbedr), intended primarily for the training of clergy. Reforming bishops were appointed, though not till 1870 was there a Welsh-speaking bishop. The contribution of the Anglican clergy and laity must not be underestimated over the whole of this period. It was Anglican clergy who had researched into early Welsh literature and made it available in print. They were taking the lead in the growing eisteddfod movement. It was members of the established church who provided most of the money for the new university college at Aberystwyth, whatever the inspiration for its founding may have been. Above all they were founding day schools, and by the mid-nineteenth century church schools were teaching the enormous majority of the population. The Chapels woke to this and fought back with their own school movement, though even by 1870, when state provision took over, their schools were still in the minority. This situation bred a twofold sense of injustice: first because the chapel families resented having to send their children to church schools; secondly because of their conviction that most of the old endowments that supported education on the church side had been given for the benefit of the whole population, and were now being used to support schools that the bulk of the population did not wish to use. This imbalance in education was a further pressure towards a disestablishment that would bring with it a redistribution of these funds.

The revitalizing of the Established church in the nineteenth century, the faithful ministry in the Welsh language of many clergy over the years, together with their huge service to the survival of the language is all part of a largely hidden history - together with that of the non-worshipping 50%. During the last half of the nineteenth century the Chapels held a near monopoly of the printed word in Welsh and it is the picture given by Chapel ministers and lay leaders that prevails as the truth about Wales at that time, sanctifying a particular kind of culture.

Only gradually did this become a political and nationalistic consciousness. For a long time the famous entry in the Encyclopedia Brittanica 'Wales: see England' was largely apt. But as the nineteenth century drew to its end, Wales became much more conscious of itself as a nation, and as a people with a history and culture of its own. Politically the change was signalled by it becoming a great Liberal stronghold. From Welsh Liberalism came one of the great Prime Ministers of the twentieth century, a leader in peace, and then supremely in the First World War, David Lloyd George. After the end of that war in 1918 Wales entered a devastating period of economic and social suffering. As a result of this, from the 1920's, there took place another great political change. Wales asserted its difference by becoming a Socialist stronghold, returning Labour members to Parliament consistently in almost every constituency till the 1970s.

It was the Liberals who were eventually to disestablish the Church. A series of measures were debated in Parliament for some 20 years until the passing of the Disestablishment Measure of 1914, which did not come into effect until after the War in 1920. The fight over disestablishment was bitter both during the period of the parliamentary struggle and afterwards and the issue distracted the churches from more important matters for at least 40 years. With disestablishment came disendowment. The money was allocated to the counties to fulfil its original social and charitable purposes for the whole population. It is now generally agreed that the effect on what became 'The Church in Wales' was good. It became a more visibly Welsh body, with at last an Archbishop of Wales, chosen from the six diocesan bishops. It provides a bilingual ministry wherever it is needed, and is now in many places standing up to the problems of the later twentieth century better than the Chapels.

The Present

The chapel buildings still dominate the towns and villages of Wales. With a number of honourable exceptions, it is small, mostly aging congregations that worship within them. They remain fiercely independent even though everything cries out for a great movement towards unity. They largely retain a travelling ministry. The minister himself is in his own chapel only on the first Sunday in the month; he spends the rest of the month fulfilling engagements in other chapels up and down the land, often returning to the same chapel on the same Sunday year after year. The problem is two-fold. First, ministers are now few and still dimishing in number - yet another argument for combining congregations: and secondly, the change which is so desperately needed, and which would most naturally come as individual congregations ventured under the guidance of ministers with vision, is stifled by the continual exchange of pulpits. Each denomination would need to be renewed entire and all at once - in human terms an almost impossible enterprise. Thus the Chapels are fossilized, not least in their worship. Not that the Chapels have a liturgical form of worship: if they had it could be debated and changed as the Church in Wales has shown in its liturgical reforms since the Second World War. Nothing, however, is so permanent as a 'free' order of worship which has solidified into a custom. Hope lies in the Sunday Schools where groups of keen lay people are able to work regularly together towards renewal in worship. This clearly is happening in places, but on the whole the Sunday School movement is also moribund, so much so that the movement has been ready to admit it and to appoint specialist workers to concentrate on rebuilding it.

There do exist movements towards cooperation between the Churches in Wales. The 'Five denominations' speak together on some issues, that is the Calvinistic Methodists - now officially The Presbyterian Church of Wales, - Congregationalists, Baptists, Weslyan Methodists and the Church in Wales. (The Roman Catholic Church is tiny in Wales, though growing.) There is a Council of Churches for Wales, the Commission of Covenanted Churches (who have signed an agreement to seek unity), and the Free Church Council (which speaks for the Chapels). These are now grouped together in an organization called *Cytun* (Christnogion ymlaen tuag at undeb - Christians forward towards unity).

There is still, however, in many places a large divide between 'Church' and 'Chapel' however much individuals now meet on friendly terms. It is a natural reaction of a minority, especially one that feels persecuted, to close ranks and to retreat into an extreme position. This happened in the Church in Wales during the period of disestablishment. It now holds a largely 'High Church' theology, without realizing much of the time that this does not reflect the wide spectrum of opinion across the border in the Church of England. As the generation that fought disestablishment has died out, a more ecumenical approach has appeared, though leaders of vision can still find themselves isolated. More sad is the refusal of chapels to come together even when they stand not more than a few yards from each other, and shelter a mere handful of worshippers in a cold and decaying building. Such is the shortage of ministers that they will often accept a preacher from another denomination. What they will not do is to move readily out of their own building to join him for exactly the same worship with another congregation.

As for the contribution of the Chapels to modern Wales, it is perhaps best for a Welshman to speak:

> The influence of the nonconformist chapels upon modern Wales will always generate controversy. Without doubt, the impact of a peculiarly sombre Sabbatarian puritanism stifled many aspects of the national genius. The chapels frowned on cultural experiment, especially in literature or the dramatic arts. They were largely immune to new currents of thought, hermetically sealed by the pressures of the Welsh language. Darwinian biology, the 'higher criticism' of modern biblical scholarship, the 'new theology' at the turn of the century made scant impact on the chapels, their denominational assemblies or *cyrddau mawr* (big meetings), their *sêt fawr* (literally 'big seat', the enclosed space around the pulpit where the lay officials of the chapel sit) of respectable middle-class shopkeepers or Lib-Lab artisans each Sunday. Nonconformity interacted closely with a ferociously zealous temperance movement: the Good Templars and the Blue Ribbon movements produced much excitement in the

eighteen seventies and eighties, while 'taking the pledge' became almost a rite of civic initiation for young schoolboys. At its worst, Welsh nonconformity helped generate tensions, frustrations and fantasies, feelings of subconscious guilt, and sexual deprivation . . . . In important respects, then, Welsh nonconformity restricted and stunted the national growth. Yet in many other ways, too, it must surely have enabled a poor, isolated, semi-feudal community to reach out for new aspirations and to fulfil itself the more completely. With all its limitations, nonconformity was responsible for almost every significant and worthwhile aspect of social and cultural activity in late nineteenth-century Wales. The preacher-poet had become a national symbol of cultural vitality (later supplanted by the professor-poet). The astonishingly rich local community life, the choral festivals, the 'penny readings', *eisteddfodau* in abundance, the wide range of Welsh- and English-language publications, much of the educational provision afforded in Sunday schools or in chapel-dominated Board elementary schools after the passage of the Forster Act in 1870, more ambitious institutions such as the 'college by the sea' founded on the coast at Aberystwyth in 1872 - the first higher education institution created in Wales apart from the exclusively Anglican college at Lampeter - all these were the creations of the chapels. More important still, the chapels lent to the Welsh national movements of the *fin de siècle* a focus for collective aspiration and action, opportunities for democratic leadership and for social mobility, most of all a self-confidence and a passion for popular education and improvement which represent much of the best of modern Wales. Ultimately, one supects, the 'big guns' of the pulpit gained their mass appeal not from the theological or the literary content of their fiery sermons but from the populist impact of their own personalities. They were accessible embodiments of that relatively classless ethos valued by Welsh-speaking people which the concept of *y werin* (the common folk) only misleadingly conveys. Below the veneer of upper-class ascendancy maintained by the landed gentry at so many levels in the eighties, the Welsh democracy was a thriving and creative one. It was nonconformist leadership and ideology that largely made it so. (Kenneth Morgan: *Rebirth of a Nation - Wales 1880-1980* pp17-18)

Being a Chapel Member

What was the ideal life for the faithful Christian at the height of the influence of the Chapel?

Life reached its climax on Sunday, the Sabbath, which was to be kept with great strictness: in the home no work was to be done, the only reading was to be of a devotional kind, the only music hymns at the piano or harmonium. The sacred hours were ten, two and six. 10.0 a.m. and 6.0 p.m. were the times for the *Oedfa,* the appointment or meeting time: or, as sometimes announced *Moddion* (that is *Moddion gras* the means of grace), or more straighforwardly *Pregeth,* the sermon, this being the chief event of the service and indeed of the Sunday. These services took place in the chapel, whose chief furnishing, apart from the close-set pews, was and is the pulpit, surrounded by the *sêt fawr,* the big seat, the enclosure in which sit the elders or deacons (according to the nomenclatures of the various denominations) who are the lay leaders of the congregation. There might be an organ behind the pulpit with seats for a choir on either side, but as like as not there is a harmonium in front of it, where the player can respond to the signals of the *codwr canu,* the 'raiser of the singing' or 'precentor' or 'cantor'. He is one of the elders who leads the singing, for which all stand, with those in the big seat turning to face the congregation. The singing is in four parts, with everyone singing their own part from the full music editions in Tonic-sol-fa. All sit and bow the head for prayer, which the minister leads *extempore,* or as the Welsh has it *o'r frest,* from the heart. The prayer is often quite extended, up to 20 minutes being possible, as the minister pleads with God for the salvation of his flock, with probably very little mention of the world and its more secular needs and problems. In the course of the morning service the children come forward to recite their verse of scripture: *dweud adnod,* saying a verse could be the highpoint of the child's week - or a weekly torment. The climax, what all have come to hear, is the sermon which can often be intensely dramatic, with the preacher at emotional high-points breaking into the *hwyl,* a kind of incanta- tional or sing-song style of delivery. The congregation may re- spond to the preacher's points, the members of the big seat being especially free with 'Amen' and 'Halleluia', or in recent times with less explicit grunts of approval. The giants of the pulpit in the great days would arrange their effects carefully, ensuring that the oil lamps were so placed that they cast great shadows of the preacher on the wall behind them. The story is told that one preacher, when giving his great sermon on 'The sheep and the goats', would find the gallery on his left gradually emptying as his congregation moved over to his right side to be with the sheep.

The preaching is the high point not only of the service but of the week and is the subject of talk on Monday when the men meet over their food in the quarry huts or at the mine or factory. In the days before radio and television the preacher is the star performer. He arrives on Saturday to be put up and entertained with due solemnity by families from the congregation deemed fit for such a privilege, often eating apart from the family in the front room or parlour, a place never sullied by ordinary family use.

On the Sunday afternoon at 2.0 p.m. old and young alike attend Sunday School, either in the 'Vestry', the hall adjacent to the Chapel or, more uncomfortably, in the Chapel itself, to work over the syllabus (*maes llafur,* the field of work) set for the year and published in text books appropriate to each age group.

The week is structured too, and thus dedicated. There is above all the *seiat,* the society meeting (the word is simply the middle syllable of the English word). This is an intimate meeting of the committed members of the chapel at which sins could be con- fessed and experiences shared. Though the minister is judged chiefly by his preaching, it is his skill in conducting the *seiat* which can contribute most to the spiritual maturity of his people. Thus a well-conducted *seiat* was and still can be a centre of growth; run to seed the *seiat* was and is a centre of hypocrisy. There is a children's *seiat* too. There might be a prayer meeting, with all expected to take part in extempore prayer or by giving out a hymn or reciting a verse.

The chapel too was the centre of cultural life. There would be a monthly meeting of the literary society with lectures fostering an interest in Welsh literature and history. Within the village, if not within the individual chapel, and meeting in the various chapels there would be choirs, a ladies' choir, a male voice choir, a mixed choir, with the annual performance of *Messiah* as the high point of its activity, all of course singing from Tonic-sol-fa.

Occasionally there would be a *noson lawen* (literally 'a happy evening'), an evening of entertainment, with singing and recitation, story-telling with appropriate expression and gesture being much prized. There would however be no dancing, and such drama as was allowed was of the most moralistic nature. All would be liberally lubricated with cups of tea, for total abstinence from alcohol had become an important part of the Christan way of life. Not that public houses did not beckon on the way to and from chapel, but they were offically frequented only by church people (the established church that is) and unbelievers, that hidden 50% that was so conveniently forgotten, though many were the rumours of the visits to the back door by staunch chapel elders or deacons to obtain supplies for home consumption.

At its best this was a classless society, proud to see its children becoming ministers and teachers, products which for a century Wales overproduced, to fill vacant posts in the English cities, and to supply leadership for the Welsh Societies, churches and chapels that flourished in many of them.

Reflections

The power that kept this activity going was the remembrance of Revival and the ever-present expectation of the next outburst of religious fervour. These broke out from time to time throughout the nineteenth century, sometimes in single denominations, often ignoring denominational boundaries, sweeping from district to district as the word spread. The most memorable of them was that of 1905, associated with the controversial young preacher Evan Roberts, which produced the last surge in chapel membership, a hump in a persistent graph of decline from the last years of the 19th century. Now all too often the Chapels live in the memory of those days, hoping, waiting for it all to happen again, buying collections of hymns and recordings with titles like *Swn y Jiwbili* 'The Sound of Jubilee' (the Welsh version of the Sankey and Moody hymns), and, most pathetic, *Adlais y Diwygiad*, 'Echo of the Revival'. There is a longing for the Spirit to move again, but with this the feeling that the Spirit will only be recognized if he moves in the same way as before, with great preaching and emotional hymn-singing. There are however many signs that the Church is being moved by the Spirit in other ways. The challenge to greater cooperation between the churches is being presented by some leaders in Wales. It is sometimes refused out of a sense of hurt remaining from past controversies. More often it is ignored out of a sense of loyalty to a great past and a feeling of weakness in a present in which all the available energy has to be expended on keeping what is there in some way alive. Meanwhile the number of ministers diminishes. Fewer and fewer villages have a resident minister. Such ministers as there are find it impossible to keep up the weekly programmes of all the chapels for which they are responsible. A great Christian culture is dying.

The year 1988, which saw the 400th anniversary of the first complete Bible in Welsh, saw also the first complete modern translation *Y Beibl Cymraeg Newydd.* Such is the feeling for the Bible that remains in Wales that large numbers have been sold. Many will have gone to homes where it cannot realistically be said to be understood; it will have been purchased for purely sentimental reasons. In others it will be understood, but no longer read as the Bible once was. Its translators hope and pray that there will be a remnant who will read and understand and act, not simply to revive an old culture but to bring new Christian life to a culture that, in its secular forms, is still very much alive and needs once more to discover its Christian roots.

Chapter 4

THE HYMNS

THE HYMNS

The Welsh word for hymn, 'emyn', appears for the first time in the l4th century, but there were hymns in Wales long before then. A monk was writing words of praise to God somewhere around 1200 in the famous *Black Book of Carmarthen*, probably the earliest surviving Welsh manuscript. All the poetry in that book is poetry with a purpose, so that these hymns were no abstract exercises but had a devotional purpose. There were hymns written to the Virgin in the following centuries, but these like the earlier hymns must have been for private use. There was no popular hymnody such as exists today.

That is not to say that the Welsh did not sing. The most famous reference to singing in Wales is in the account given by Gerald the Welshman (?1146-1223, Giraldus Cambrensis). In 1188 he traveled round Wales with Baldwin, Archbishop of Canterbury, who was preaching the first Crusade. He wrote an account of that journey in which he speaks of trumpets and pipes and of entertainment in the evenings by the harp, pipes and a stringed instrument called the *crowd* or *crwth*. His most tantalizing words however are in a later book, *The Description of Wales:*

> When they come together to make music, the Welsh sing their traditional songs, not in unison, as is done elsewhere, but in parts, in many modes and modulations. When a choir gathers to sing, which happens often in this country, you will hear as many different parts and voices as there are performers, all joining together in the end to produce a single organic harmony and melody in the soft sweetness of B-flat.

One is tempted to see here the beginnings of that singing in harmony which has become so distinctive of Welsh congregational singing. Certainly the singing continued in the great houses of the land. There is a vigorous account of Christmas revelry from the pen of Dafydd Bach ap Madog Wladaidd (f1.1340-1390) two hundred years later. There, in his patron's hall he found:

Many a minstrel and merry fiddler,
 And much the mirth on a polished floor,
And the sound of strings, a deluge of drinks,
And the constant cadence of singing.
 (trans. Joseph P. Clancy)

This willingness to sing was not taken up into Christian worship until the Reformation, and in this as in other respects, the effects were slow to reach Wales. Following the publication of the *Book of Common Prayer* in Welsh and of the whole Bible in Welsh in 1588, thoughts of Welsh men began to turn to the need for a metrical psalter in Welsh. This had already come into being in English. The work had begun under Edward VI, and continued at greater pace in the reign of Mary Tudor among the English Puritans in exile in Holland and above all in Switzerland. It came into full flower on their return at the accession of Elizabeth I in 1558. In an important book of 1595 on the nature of the Church of England, Maurice Kyffin (1555-98) wrote of the need for a Welsh metrical psalter. In the same year a number of metrical psalms were published by Thomas Middleton, one of Elizabeth's sea captains, who fought against the Spaniards. He completed his psalter on campaign in the West Indies and it was published in 1603. Sadly the traditional metres that he used were so complex that his versions were not suitable for singing. At the same time Maurice's brother Edward (1558-1603) was at work. Before his untimely death of the plague in 1603 he is reported as having produced 50 psalm versions. Of these we have only one copy, set for printing, of the first twelve and 5 verses of the 13th, dated 1603. It is almost certain that the work was broken off at this point by his death. In his introduction he wrote:

> Let no true Welshman give sleep to his eyes or slumber to his eyelids, as the prophet David said, until he has seen the glory of the Lord, by facilitating the completion of this godly task in the language of his own country.

His versions did indeed prepare the way for a much more important work *The Book of Psalms (Llyfr y Psalmau)* by Archdeacon Edmwnd Prys (1544-1623), published in 1621. Most of the psalms are in a particularly Welsh version of the Long Metre and Common Metre family of ballad metres known as the 'Psalm

Metre' (*Mesur Salm*). H.W.Baker's version of Psalm 23 is the most familiar example of this meter in most current English hymn-books:

> The King of love my shepherd is.
>   whose goodness faileth never;
> I nothing lack if I am his
>   and he is mine for ever.

This example shows that the metre depends on the feminine ending in lines 2 and 4, which is difficult to handle in English but common in Welsh since so very many of the words are regularly accented on the last syllable but one. Edmwnd Prys produced a very fine version of the Psalms, better than any in English and certain of them have remained in almost constant use till today. Some of the great 19th century preachers made very effective use of them and they undoubtedly have their place in worship alongside the more emotional hymns written since.

Little was published in the 17th century that can be given the name of hymnody. There was the work of the Reverend Rhys Prichard (1579?-1644). His *Cannwyll y Cymry* (*The Candle of the Welsh*), from which came the delightful carol 'Come to Bethlehem' (see page 34), was not published until some years after his death. His simple, moral verses can hardly be called hymns, but nevertheless they were the only Welsh source used by John Gambold in his *Hymns of the Children of God in all ages* 1754.

The Puritans were divided in their attitude to hymn singing, but in Wales one of the great leading figures, Vavasor Powell (1617-1670), was advocating public hymn singing in an epistle to the churches in the Commonwealth period. Among the Welsh Puritans Vavasor Powell wrote hymns in English and Morgan Llwyd (1619-59) in Welsh. In the mid 17th century there were some members of the Established Church who were were prepared to go beyond the metrical psalms and to sing hymns, but not in any systematic way. In the 1662 revision of the *Book of Common Prayer* there was, as in earlier versions, only one hymn, the 'Veni Creator Spiritus' in the Ordination Service; in the new book this appeared in a new English version by John Cosin 'Come, Holy Ghost, our souls inspire'. Thus when a Welsh translation of the new Prayer Book was produced in 1664 a new Welsh translation was needed, and that of Rowland Fychan (Rowland Vaughan c1590-1667) was used.

The serious publication of hymns in Welsh began, however, with the work of Thomas Baddy (date of birth uncertain, probably in the 1670's, died 1729) a Presbyterian minister in Denbigh. He added 'Six Scriptural Hymns on the Sacrament' to a translation of a work on the Sacrament which he published in 1703. In the light of the way that church life developed in later periods it may seem strange that these early hymns are on this subject. There was however a double point to this: there is scriptural warranty in that Jesus and his disciples sang a hymn after the Last Supper; and further, that while many dissenters had grave doubts about the singing of God's praises by unbelievers, at the sacrament only believers would be allowed to be present. James Owen (1654-1706) published in 1705 *Hymnau Scrythurol (Scriptural Hymns, with particular emphasis on the Sacraments of the Lord's Supper and of Baptism)*. His book was reprinted after his death in 1717 with considerable additions. These hymns must have seen considerable use since later collections include them and they appear in various manuscript collections made by exhorters to be sung in meetings of the Methodist Societies.

In the 1710 reprint of the *Book of Common Prayer* there appeared a funeral hymn 'Myfi yw'r Atgyfodiad mawr' by Ellis Wynne (1670/1-1734), author of one of the great prose works of the period *Gweledigaethau y Bardd Cwsc (Visions of the Sleeping Bard)*. His hymn still survives in the hymnbooks and must be accounted the earliest true hymn to do so.

> "The Resurrection and the Life
>   Am I" the Lord declareth,
> And for all those who trust in Him
>   Eternal life prepareth.
>
> "A welcome in the heavenly home
>   Is waiting for whoever
> Obediently will serve me here
>   And Death shall harm him never."
>
> "In truth, in truth," says Truth himself,
>   "All men on earth who hear me
> And trust in Him who sent me here
>   Shall live for ever near me."

"And everyone who strives his best
In faith my words to follow
Shall not be judged, but onward pass
From death to glorious morrow."
(translated M.J.H.Ellis)

In 1725 there appeared a further small collection by Thomas Baddy, which was reprinted with additions in 1740, and in the intervening years there were collections by various Independent ministers who ventured into this still new enterprise of writing hymns for congregations to sing. The title pages and the hymns themselves make it clear that they are still more than a little hesitant to move far from scripture, and many are still written to be sung after the Sacrament. Some were more skilful than others in their handling of the limited number of metres then in use, (Long, Common and Psalm Metre). Of them all it can be said that there was little of the fire that was soon to come. In general this hymnody was a fair reflection of church life at the time. Much of it was slack and uninspired. But the very existence of the hymns reflects the fact that there was in many places a devoted ministry, whether among the dissenters or in the Established Church, and a searching for new and better things. The new life came with the Methodist Revival, but it did not give immediate birth to a new hymnody. There was still some preparing of the ground to be done. What did come almost immediately was a realization of how important singing could be in the life of the newly founded Societies. Following his conversion experience at Easter and Whitsun 1735, Howell Harris began his work of exhortation, preaching and prayer. He also started to form groups of new-born Christians with the intention that they should adopt a common rule of life and assist one another by word and example in the leading of the Christian life. By December 1736 Harris was in the company of John Games, a singer from Talgarth, who was a travelling teacher of psalm singing. Together they visited 'Y Wernos' a farm in the parish of Llandyfalle, and there the first true 'Society' was founded — *Seiat* as the word soon became in Welsh. The teaching of singing and the founding of the *seiat* went together. From this date onwards there are many references in Harris's voluminous diaries to hymns and psalms and to singing. In January 1738 we find him soaked to the skin on the road between Ystrad-ffin and Llanwrtyd and feeling none of this because he was singing psalms on the way. He refers to a hymn on the sacrament, of which he quotes a verse, and to a hymn of Vavasor Griffiths. His most tantalizing reference is in January 1741. He writes there of his hearing in September 1740 a young minister in Llanwrtyd giving out a hymn to be sung and of his being sent into a spiritual ecstasy by it. William Williams was in Llanwrtyd in September 1740. It is possible that he was the young minister who was introducing the hymn on the theme of 'God's good will to receive all' to which Harris refers. But was it his own hymn? And why does Harris not name him?

Harris himself began at this time to write hymns. He first made a translation of a Moravian hymn which John Wesley had translated from the German as 'Shall I, for fear of feeble man' and published in 1739. Harris' hymn ended with a translation of Bishop Ken's doxology, 'Praise God from whom all blessings flow'. This is the only verse by Harris that survives in the hymn-books, but it is the standard version of these words in Welsh. The whole hymn was published in 1740 in a small collection of thirteen hymns by various hands. Only one of them is known today, and that is by the Reverend Gruffydd Jones of Llanddowror himself, a harvest hymn 'O Arglwydd Dduw'r cynhaeaf mawr' (O Lord, the God of the great harvest). A verse at the end of the booklet promises a full-sized book of three hundred hymns; this never appeared, but the promise shows at least that there was thought to be a great deal of material to hand and a considerable demand for it.

As with other aspects of Daniel Rowland's life we know less of his development in this field, but there was a hymn by him in a book published in 1740 containing a mixture of hymns, an essay on the Song of Solomon (a reprint of a work by Thomas Baddy) and another on the rules for organizing the 'weekly societies'. Certainly then this book was for Methodists.

In 1741 Harris bought *The Hymns and Songs of the Church* (1623) by George Wither, the book for which Orlando Gibbons wrote the tunes. It is impossible to know what influence this had on Harris, but about that time he was "making hymns" and "was led to write some hymns, I hope useful ones."

In 1742 there was held the first 'Association' of the Welsh Methodists, the *Sasiwn* as it came to be called and there the rules for the Societies were drawn up. These make it clear that the custom was to sing a hymn at the beginning of the Society meeting. Together with the rules was published the first official collection of hymns for the Methodist Societies, possibly following the example of Charles Wesley who already had published *Hymns and Sacred Poems* in 1739 and another volume of the same name in 1740 containing some of his greatest hymns. The Welsh movement may have in this respect been outwardly in step with the English, but at this stage its hymns did not have the same quality. 'Tame' is the word that G.M. Roberts uses of them in his book on William Williams; they do not show the fire of the revival that they were intended to serve. As yet there was no standard in Welsh against which to measure them and if they were 'useful', then that had to be enough. Hymns continued to appear. In 1744 a collection of 69 appeared, 'mainly by Daniel Rowland' according to the title page. No names are given; some are known to be by Baddy and others can be ascribed to Daniel Rowland from other evidence. Indeed Rowland, though no great hymnodist, was a considerable contributor to this early flow of 'useful' hymns.

The manuscript collections are another indication of how widespread was the singing of hymns. These were copied by the exhorters, the leaders of the local societies, whose duty it was to guide the meeting and, clearly, according to the rules of 1742, to see that the meeting began with a hymn. That the hymn singing was no pale formality is clear from references in an *Anterliwt* (Interlude — a type of popular comic entertainment performed in the open air at fairs) published in 1745 by William Roberts of Llanor in the Lleyn Peninsula, with the sub-title 'The Scourge of the Methodists'. Howell Harris is portrayed instructing Siencyn Morgan (possibly the father of Dafydd Siencyn Morgan, see page 134) on how to be a success as a Methodist Exhorter:

> In the first place you must sing and shout
> Hymns by the score if you would be devout,
> Then you must frighten to death with your roar
> The people asleep in the house next door.
>
> Fools there will be just like unbridled horses,
> Snorting away as they sing through their noses,
> Turning both this way and that for to find
> The verses that send the land out of its mind.

> Then for a while they fall in with the time,
> Keeping the tune of the music in mind,
> Then they believe there was never a bird
> Singing so sweetly as they to be heard.

Then in 1744 was published a book which began to give to the hymn singing of the Methodists that poetic power combined with spiritual fire that it had so far lacked. This was *Aleluia* (*Alleluia or a Collection of Hymns on a variety of subjects*) by William Williams, Pantycelyn. There were only nine hymns, and these show Williams as still an apprentice in his craft even though they are much in advance of anything written by his contemporaries. Five more, rather larger, collections under this title were issued up to 1747; part 6 contained over 30 hymns by other writers. Many influences have been traced in *Aleluia*: Williams was learning and translating from the English writers, Cennick, Erskine, Watts and Hervey. By this means he introduced new metres into Welsh to add to the four available so far. In the end Williams was to introduce no less than 26 or 27 new metres.

William Williams, Pantycelyn

William Williams was born in early 1717, the fourth child of John Williams a Cardiganshire farmer. John had married into a prosperous family and in 1731 William's mother, Dorothy, inherited the fairly large farm of Pantycelyn, some four miles from Llandovery. It is not clear whether the family moved there immediately or later, on John's death in 1741. The family were Independents and worshipped at the chapel at Cefnarthen at first, but later moved with a Calvinistic group that broke away to set up its own meeting house. Williams intended to be a doctor and for that purpose he went to the Dissenting Academy of Llwyn-llwyd, probably attending a branch of it at Chancefield near Talgarth. Thus it was that he came to hear Howell Harris preaching in the churchyard at Talgarth in 1737 or 1738 and was converted. Williams deserted both his old background as an Independent and his first intention to become a doctor. On Harris' advice he sought ordination in the Established Church, to which of course Howell Harris belonged and within which it was the intention of its founders that the Methodist Movement should remain. He was ordained deacon in the Bishop's palace at Abergwili in August 1740, and licened to serve as curate in the parochial chapels of

Llanwrtyd and Dewi Abergwesin under the Vicar Theophilus Evans, a bitter opponent of Methodism. We hear of him preaching with fervour both within the parish and beyond. Under these circumstances it is not surprising that he was refused priest's orders. It was however a great loss to himself and to the movement. He was accused of various misdemeanours against the discipline of the church in the Bishop's court in 1742 and 1743 and in early 1744 left the parochial ministry and devoted himself to the Methodist cause.

He spent some time as a schoolmaster in the parish of Llansawel, and it was there that he met and married Mary Francis, probably in 1748. She was a good and godly woman, to judge from the accounts we have of her, brought up in the faith by Gruffydd Jones, Llanddowror. Her gifts were many: she could sing and possibly played the fiddle. Before long the newly married couple moved to Pantycelyn to join Williams' mother Dorothy, by then a widow. Mary was an heiress in her own right and the property at Pantycelyn was considerable. Thus the Williams family were by no means poor. Mary brought with her some of her gentrified tastes. She insisted on tea from teacups in Pantycelyn, and Williams came to share her liking for tea. He bought it by the chest and shared it with friends; there is even some evidence that he sold tea as a sideline. So it was that from this quiet farm in Breconshire the greatest poet and hymnwriter of his day would set out on his arduous journeys across Wales, preaching and acting as spiritual advisor to the Society meetings and to the lay 'exhorters' who led them week by week.

When and how did Williams come to write hymns? It is interesting to speculate. William Lewis, Pantycelyn, his uncle, owned a copy of George Wither's *Halleluia or Britain's Second Remembrancer* (1641) which passed to Williams and it is tempting to think of its hymns being sung at Pantycelyn and Williams taking its title for his own first collection of hymns. That these were English hymns need not surprise us. Williams was bilingual with his English somewhat more fluent and correct than his Welsh. He wrote most of his letters, for example, in English.

The usual story of his beginning to write hymns is that given by Thomas Charles of Bala, the leader of the movement in the second generation:

The first Association of the Welsh Calvinistic Methodists was held in Jeered Dafydd's house, Rhiwiau,
in the parish of Llanddeusant in the county of
Carmarthen. Present at this meeting were Mr H.
Harris, The Revd Daniel Rowland, The Revd W.
Williams and two or three exhorters. Although
small in number the meeting was greatly blessed
with the presence of the Lord. — At a morning
meeting after this, Mr Harris is said to have encouraged all that were there to compose a few verses of
poetry by the next meeting to see whether the Lord
had given the gift of poetry to one of them, and
who that was. So they did: and after they had all
read their compositions, it was decided unani-
mously that Mr W. Williams had received this excellent gift, and Mr Harris and everyone else
encouraged him to use it for the glory of God and
the good of his Church.

Another account rounds off the story with Harris pronouncing
"Williams has the singing" (*Williams piau y canu*). Yet another
version gives the words to Rowland, in character too, that joking
character that so irritated Harris, "Well, Will, the singing is yours,
at any rate."

The story is shot through with problems: the meeting is either
said to be in the wrong place or wrongly identified as the first
meeting of the Association. Then, if Williams was recognized at
that point as the so-to-speak official hymn writer of the movement, why were his hymns not in the first official collection of
1742? — the problems can be multiplied. But there are yet deeper
problems. What of that service in September 1740 in Llanwrtyd
when Harris was sent into an ecstasy by a hymn? And what of the
early collection of hymns by Williams, the only one to survive in
his own hand? This is a manuscript book which seems to have
passed from Daniel Rowland to Williams when it was half filled
with hymns, mainly in an unknown hand, after which Williams
used it to make fair copies of 55 of his earliest hymns. Two of
these were used in Part I of *Aleluia* (1744) and more in the
subsequent parts.

The dramatic scene described by Thomas Charles is rather like
that of the 12 Apostles sitting round a table and each contributing
a clause to the Apostles' Creed. It is a pious legend. It is more likely

that Williams learned and refined his art over many years. At least until 1745 it was Rowland and Harris, together with the hymn writers of Monmouthshire, who held the field. After a few years it was clear that indeed the gift belonged to William Williams, Pantycelyn. Modern hymnbooks show this; they include one hymn by Gruffydd Jones, one hymn by Rowland, the doxology translated by Harris and not a line by all those other earlier labourers, while the initial 'W' appears on almost every page.

William Williams developed slowly, but this was not only the growth of a hymn writer but of a major poet who was forging a wholly new kind of poetry. He received a sound education, but it was entirely in English. To the end of his life, even when he had developed as a great poet, his Welsh had formal weaknesses of grammar and a certain lack of discrimination in choice of words. He had not been schooled in the strict Welsh poetic tradition. Although this had by his day lost much of its vitality, there were those working to revitalize it, and he was much criticized by them for his free handling of both language and metre. Under these circumstances it was natural for him to look farther afield for models, in fact to England where the writing of hymns was fully developed and where Charles Wesley's finest hymns had already been written. It may have been these very circumstances that led him to develop a free verse style, and to become in point of fact the first Welsh romantic poet.

His development continued in *Hosanna i Fab Dafydd* (*Hosanna to the Son of David*) published in three parts 1751-1754 and later re-issued with the complete *Aleluia*. He reached maturity in 1762 with the publication of *Caniadau y rhai sydd ar y Mor o Wydr* (*Songs of those upon the Sea of Glass*), a collection of over 130 hymns after additions in 1764 and 1773 (though some of the hymns had appeared in earlier collections). *Ffarwel Weledig, Groesaw Anweledig Bethau* (*Farewell things seen. Welcome things unseen*) appeared, Part I in 1763 with 84 hymns and Part II in 1766 with 85. *Gloria in Excelsis* appeared in 1771 with 74 hymns, and a second part in 1772 with 93. There were also collections of hymns in English, *Hosanna to the Son of David* in 1759 and *Gloria in Excelsis* in 1772. Thus the great classical body of Welsh hymnody appeared in a mere ten years. Further collections followed until his death in 1791.

In his book on Williams, Glyn Tegai Hughes points out that Williams developed a theory of hymnody in his introductions to the various collections. As early as *Aleluia* part II he emphasized the need to be scriptural; hymns that are firmly based on the scriptures fix those texts in the minds of the users with the result that they work deeply on their affections or emotions. Hymns must be centred on Christ; in *Rhai Hymnau a Chaniadau Duwiol (Some Hymns and Godly Songs* 1757) he points out that he has removed 'the hateful little word 'I' and placed Jesus, his grace and his love, in its place'. No doubt arising from his own experience in congregations and societies using them he confessed that

> some of the first hymns are too exalted in their
> assurance of faith, their longing for release, their
> spiritual joy in the victory over the enemy for weak
> Christians to be able to sing them.

He therefore urges wise choice of hymns to meet the condition of the congregation. In 1766 he discussed the need for

> variety, new experiences, new light, words, expres-
> sions, meters to arouse a sense of God's love.

He advises hymn writers that they must seek true grace, and write under the inspiration of the Holy Spirit: and he advises them to read all the books of poetry they can get, in English or other languages, and above all the poetical books of the Bible, since here they find all these things. These principles can be commended to any hymn writer today.

Williams did not only write hymns. For a complete understanding of the man and of his genius his full output must be examined. He wrote longer poems including two epics. He also wrote a series of masterly elegies. The subjects of these were not only the leading figures of the movement, but also humble believers, not all of them men. In this he brought together the old Welsh traditions of the laudatory odes and the Puritan tradition of the spiritual biography. His prose works from his maturity are of great importance: he wrote on marriage in what we may find even today a remarkably 'modern' manner; he wrote on the conduct of the Societies, a subject of which he was a master.

But his great and abiding achievement lies in his hymns. It is of course in their original language that they shine most brightly, but some of their power can be seen in translation. Whatever else needs to be said about his hymns, in them he is always the saved sinner sharing his experience through his preaching and his song with his fellow Christians. As he does this he provides them through his writing with the words by which they may shape their own experience as well as express it. So, although he says that his aim in his hymns is to cut out the 'I' that once was too central, he never does this. Although he came to centre his attention more and more on Christ, he is always celebrating what Christ has done for him and so for all who may read or sing his words. This is wonderfully true in one of his greatest hymns 'Yn Eden, cofiaf hynny byth'. Here the victory of Christ is celebrated: nevertheless in both verses it is 'to me', 'for me':

'Yn Eden cofiaf hynny byth'

Can I forget bright Eden's grace,
My beauteous crown and princely place,
　　All lost, all lost to me?
Long as I live I'll praise and sing
My wondrous all-restoring King
　　Victor of Calvary.

Lo! Faith, behold the place, the tree
Whereon the Prince of Heaven, for me,
　　All innocent, was nailed;
One here has crushed the dragon's might;
Two fell, but One has won the fight;
　　Christ Jesus has prevailed.
　　　　　　　　　　　(trans. H.A.Hodges)

Williams' sense of sin is always present, though he knows that the victory has been won:

'O! golch fi beunydd'

O wash me daily, wash me clean,
　　Yea wash me Lord completely,
My hands, my heart, my head and feet,
　　Oh with thy blood now cleanse me.

Baptise me with thy spirit's power
　　Like ardent flame so fervent,

Yea purify my heart through fire,
  And o'er my sin mete judgement.

Destroy of sin each lingering trace,
  Make me, through grace, thy dwelling,
A beauteous temple, pure abode,
  God's own beloved building.
                    (trans. Miss Jane Owen)

Much has been made of Williams as a poet of nature. Indeed there is much in his hymns that comes from a keen observation of the world in the fields around Pantycelyn. It is often possible to see Williams' own native land in his hymns, that land that he traversed so many times in his preaching journeys and in his visits to the society meetings that he could so skilfully guide. An English hymn begins with a view of the Black mountains from Pantycelyn:

O'er those gloomy hills of darkness
  Look, my soul, be still and gaze;
All the promises do travail
  With a glorious day of grace.
    Blessed jubil, blessed jubil,
  Let thy glorious morning dawn.

This is one of the first 'missionary hymns', with the overseas mission of the church exciting the imagination of one who knew well the blessings received in the mission field at home. Verse six is clear enough:

Fly abroad, eternal Gospel,
  Win and conquer, never cease;
May thy eternal wide dominions
  Multiply, and still increase;
    May thy sceptre, may thy sceptre
  Sway th' enlightened world around.

But his world is a mixture of his own Wales and the land of the Bible. So a preaching journey can become both the toiling of the Israelites through the wilderness and Everyman's pilgrimage through life to the eternal home. The best known of his hymns in English, 'Guide me, 0 thou great Jehovah', shows the truth of this;

in it we are the Israelites seeking food and water in the wilderness and at the end we are passing through the waters of the Jordan to reach final safety on the other side. So too in the last verse of his missionary hymn the geography of the Bible intrudes:

> O let Moab yield and tremble,
>   Let Philistia never boast,
> And let India proud be scattered
>   With its innumerable host;
>   And the glory, and the glory,
>   Jesus, only be to thee.

Some of his hymns are true love songs to his beloved, his Saviour, using often the imagery of the *Song of Songs*. Again in an English hymn:

> White and ruddy is my Beloved

he begins, in a phrase that sounds well when he uses it in Welsh, and when his successors borrow it, but is difficult in English. He continues in verse three:

> Such as found thee found such sweetness,
>   Deep, mysterious, and unknown;
> Far above all worldly pleasures,
>   If they were to meet in one;
>   My beloved, my beloved,
>   O'er the mountains haste away.

In a different metre he uses the same source:

> O my beloved! haste away,
> Thy gracious coming don't delay,
>   Leap o'er the hills like a young roe;
> O meet a soul in mournful pain,
> My peace, my joys, let me regain,
>   And be my God where'er I go.

More powerfully in Welsh he begins with the same theme, and continues with another which is often to be found in his hymns, the longing to leave the worthless things of this life and to be with God:

100

'Rwy'n edrych, dros y bryniau pell'

I gaze across the distant hills,
    Thy coming to espy;
Beloved, haste, the day grows late,
    The sun sinks down the sky.

All the old loves I followed once
    Are now unfaithful found;
But a sweet sickness holds me yet
    Of love that has no bound!

Love that the sensual heart ne'er knows,
    Such power, such grace it brings,
Which sucks desire and thought away
    From all created things.

O make me faithful while I live,
    Attuned but to thy praise,
And may no pleasure born of earth
    Entice to devious ways.

All my affections now withdraw
    From objects false, impure,
To the one object which unchanged
    Shall to the last endure.

There is no station under heaven
    Where I have lust to live;
Only the mansions of God's house
    Can perfect pleasure give.

Regard is dead and lust is dead
    For the world's gilded toys;
Her ways are nought but barrenness,
    And vain are all her joys.
                    (trans. H Idris Bell)

Here the longing for the life to come is wistful, with that typically Welsh quality of *hiraeth,* a longing for what is not present that can often sap the energy, and can be mere nostalgia. But for Williams there is also the note of triumph, of the goal all but gained, the pilgrimage completed, the battle won under the leadership of the one who first fought his way through from death to life for us:

'Marchog, Iesu, yn llwyddiannus'

Ride on, Jesus, all victorious,
  Bear thy sword upon thy side;
None on earth can e'er withstand thee,
  Nor yet hell, for all its pride:
At thy mighty name tremendous
  Every foe is forced to yield;
Hushed in awe, creation trembles:
  Come then, Jesus, take the field.

Rescue now our souls from bondage,
  In the morn of victory,
Batter down the doors of Babel,
  Break the bars and set us free:
Let thy rescued hosts, exulting,
  Troop to freedom, wave on wave,
Like the surge of mighty waters:
  O come quickly, come and save!

Hark I hear already, faintly,
  Songs of vict'ry from afar,
Where the heirs of thy redemption
  Hail thy triumph in the war.
Clad in robes of shining glory,
  Palms of conquest in each hand,
Joyful hosts, to freedom marching,
  Enter now the promised land.
                    (trans. G. O. Williams)

Before 1762 the revival had flowed, however powerfully, along narrow channels. From then on it swept forward, much in the spirit of this hymn, with Williams' hymns both setting the movement forward with great power and giving the newly converted the language in which to express their new-found faith. It would seem that all revivals need their song. Williams' contemporaries in England were fortunate in having in Charles Wesley a great poet. Some more recent revivals have had to make do with rather trivial material. The Welsh were indeed blessed in that at the heart of their revival was a poet of towering genius.

The Contemporaries of William Williams, Pantycelyn

The flow of hymns that had begun before William Williams, Pantycelyn began to publish did not stop. Wales did not stand and hold its breath as this new giant was formed in its midst. It would have been most surprising if it had, since Wales had been for centuries, as it is even now, a land where poetry is a natural form of utterance. That is not to say that no notice was taken of Williams in his time. His mark is everywhere, above all in the free verse that he gave to the language. This became the almost universal utterance for the hymn and was gladly taken up by many of his contemporaries.

Dafydd Jones, Caio (1710 or 1711-1777)

Little is known of the antecedents of Dafydd (Davit) Jones, Caio. The district around Caio, a village in Carmarthenshire not far from Pantycelyn, was well provided with good schools at that time. From his early days he followed the typical pattern of the village poet and wrote verses, comic and serious about his own life and what went on around him. On his wedding day he wrote of his ride to his new home:

> The old grey horse is a-creaking
> And sweat from his side is dripping,
> Bearing the load of wife and man
> All the way to Cwmgogerddan.

He took part in that constant trade of cattle from Wales to the markets of England, and especially London. One Sunday he was on his way home from one such journey when he heard the sound of singing from the old Independent chapel of Troedrhiwdalar. He went in, listened to the sermon and was converted, and on his reaching home he joined the Independents (Congregationalists) in Crugybar. There has been a natural tendency to play down the spiritual strength of the Independents in the years before the Methodist Revival, but there were a number of shining lights who were to prove supportive to Methodists and 1735 was a turning point for them all.

Dafydd Jones had probably heard the congregation singing the psalms of Edmwnd Prys. Fine though these are they had in them too little of the Gospel for the newly awakened Christians. Some of the Dissenting ministers supported the new movement. Most of those in the tradition of Dissent however (the Dry Dissenters as they were known), tended to look down on the emotionalism of the new movement and its uproarious hymn singing, but they did recognize the need for a middle way. That was found in the Christianized psalm versions of Isaac Watts. Who better to translate them than a skilful poet, now a devout Christian, who was thoroughly familiar with English both from his schooling and by reason of his constant journeyings across the border? Dafydd Jones' translations from Watts' *Psalms* were published in 1753, and he says in his introduction that he undertook the work on the urging of certain Reverend Ministers. In 1775 was published his translation of Watts' *Hymns and Spiritual Songs*. Dafydd Jones is on the whole a successful translator. Something is always lost in translation and Dafydd Jones ties his own hands somewhat by retaining the metres of the original. But for the most part there is no sign that these are translations, they run so naturally as Welsh.

Dafydd Jones wrote original hymns too, some of which are standard in all the hymnbooks since his day. It is impossible to give in English the quality of his translations of Watts; one would have simply to reprint Watts. Here however are verses from one of his original hymns:

'Dewch, frodyr, un fryd'

Come, brethren, unite
In holy delight,
To praise our Beloved — redemption's great light:
How sweet is the care
His love to declare —
That he should our chastisement faithfully bear.

A poor man he came,
Enduring our shame,
To be our redeemer — our brother by name:
Declare his renown,
The rights of his crown —
His life for the sheep hath the Shepherd laid down.
(trans. H. Elvet Lewis 1860-1953)

Morgan Rhys (1716-79)

'A man without history' is how Evan Isaac describes Morgan Rhys in his book on the chief hymn writers of Wales. That may be so, but his hymns are in constant use. He wrote far fewer than Williams Pantycelyn, but certainly in the earlier years of this century they were sung much more frequently. Such of his life as is known comes from the references to him in *Welch Piety* the annual report of the progress of the circulating Schools that Gruffydd Jones provided for his subscribers. He worked in the schools from 1757-1775 and it is clear from the letters about him that Gruffydd Jones transcribes that his work with both children and adults was deeply appreciated. It is possible that he was a preacher and exhorter with the Methodists. We do not know this for sure; it would have been against the rules of the Circulating Schools, which were loyal to the Established Church, though these rules were less strictly observed afther the death of Gruffydd Jones in 1761. There is a tradition that for the last years of his life Morgan Rhys kept his own private school in Capel Isaac, a village between Llanfynnydd and Llandeilo. His Will makes it clear that by then at least his spiritual home was in the Methodist society meeting. He was buried in the churchyard at Llanfynnydd on August 9th 1779, but in keeping with his life the place of his grave is unknown.

His hymns certainly prove him to have been in spirit very much part of the Methodist Revival. He clearly breathes the same air as the great preachers. His work proves him to be one of the truly great spirits of that time.

His place in the history of Welsh poetry and piety rests entirely on his collections of hymns, since they rise far above his other writings. In 1755 he published *View from Mount Nebo of the Promised Land* (*Golwg o Ben Nebo*), with eleven hymns. A number of other small collections followed. Like some other hymn writers (including William Williams himself) he was not a great craftsman: there are weaknesses in metre and rime, in his use of the language and in the quality of his imagery. But he has great originality both in metre and content; he never adapts or translates. There is a balance in his hymns between the sins and troubles of God's people and their joys and triumphs, though perhaps there is too much emphasis on the former for modern taste. His hymns have a considerable intellectual and moral strength as well as strong feeling. There is a tradition that from time to time he read his hymns to William Williams, Pantycelyn, who once responded in his blunt way: 'Well you've got the experience of a good Christian and a half there!'.

Here is a hymn that, unusually in Welsh, takes its starting point in the Christmas story:

> 'Peraidd ganodd sêr y bore'

> All the morning stars were singing
>   When the King of Heaven was born;
> Wise men journeyed to adore him,
>   Shepherds too, that happy morn:
>   Precious treasure, precious treasure,
>   In the manger Jesus lay.

> For the lost he is a Saviour,
>   And the bruised be maketh whole;
> Ever loveth he to pardon
>   The poor sinful, erring soul:
>   Praise him ever, praise him ever;
>   To the dust of earth he came.
>   *(trans. Miss Jane Owen)*

The theme of salvation is never far from the mind of these early Methodists, its wonder, the sheer amazing wonder of it.

It is, however, sometimes expressed in a self centred way. One reason for the constant use of Morgan Rhys' hymns may well be that although he knows that this salvation is indeed for him, he can point away from himself to the objective reality of what Christ has done.

> 'O! agor fy llygaid i weled'

> Lord, open mine eyes to behold
>   The worth of thy wondrous decree:
> Far better than silver and gold,
>   The law of thy mouth is to me:
> The fire shall consume all below,
>   But thou art the same, and thy plan —
> 'Tis life everlasting to know
>   My saviour as God and as Man.

O wonder of infinite cost!
  The way that he took in his grace,
To rescue a man that was lost,
  By dying himself in his place!
He conquered the serpent's despite,
  And stood there alone as my King!
He leadeth us now in his might —
  Let those on the rock shout and sing.

The mighty one has overcome,
  His foes in confusion retire;
And Zion is on its way home
  In terrible chariots of fire;
The saints and the angels unite,
  A white-shining numberless throng,
To bear through the realms of the light,
  To him the all-conquering song.
(trans. H. Elvet Lewis)

David William, Llandeilo Fach (1720/1-1794)

Again little is known of the life of David (or Dafydd) William, but tradition has it that he was a tailor. We hear of his preaching with the Methodists and then in about 1746 leaving both tailoring and preaching to become a teacher in the circulating schools. We also hear of problems in his marriage. His wife had a strong will of her own and insisted on keeping a tavern. David William was disciplined by his church because of this, and left to become a Baptist; this apparently happened in 1777. That year he covenanted with 13 others to found a church in Croes-y-Parc, and there he stayed as a member and as assistant preacher for the rest of his life.

There is a story told of how he came to write his most famous hymn. One Sunday he had been preaching some distance away from home. He returned through wind and rain only to find that his sharp-tongued wife had bolted the door and gone to bed. When she proved deaf to his pleas he turned for shelter to the cowshed where he could hear, above the pounding of the rain on the roof, the roaring of the river Llwchwr in torrent.

'Yn y dyfroedd mawr a'r tonnau'

In the waves and mighty waters
  No one will support my head,
But my Saviour, my beloved,
  Who was stricken in my stead:
In the cold and mortal river
  He will hold my head above;
I shall through the waves go singing
  For one look of him I love.

(trans. H. Elvet Lewis)

John Thomas, Rhaeadr Gwy (1730-1804?)

John Thomas was a minor figure, but his long life conveniently spans the last years of the founding fathers of the Revival and the rise of the second generation. Of necessity this period can be seen in two ways. It was a time of diminishing fervour and greater formality; but it was also a time of consolidation, when one of the great Welsh religious institutions, the Sunday School, was founded and established.

He himself grew up with the Revival. He went into service in a godly household, was converted by the preaching of Howell Harris, joined the local congregational church, and then went of his own choosing at the age of 15 to be a servant in the household of Gruffydd Jones, hoping to receive advice and education to help him to be a preacher. Of very small stature and with no education he must have appeared an unpromising candidate to Gruffydd Jones and so two years later he went to Howell Harris' school at Trevecca, and after a year there went to keep a school himself in Llanfigan, Breckonshire, where he began to preach. So began a period of his life during which he moved from one place to another as schoolmaster and preacher. In 1761 he became once again a member of the Congregational Church and after four years training he was ordained in 1767 as minister of Rhaeadr Gwy. He had great success as minister in his own church but also continued to travel around the country as an evangelist more in the manner of the Methodists than the Congregationalists. In 1794 he settled again as schoolmaster and preacher.

He was the first to write hymns in Welsh for children. His hymns are uneven in inspiration, but his best have been very servicable. This has been sung at many a funeral:

'Am fod fy Iesu'n byw'

> Because my Jesus rose
> So too his saints shall rise,
> Though each one pain and suffering knows
>   Great is their prize;
> Through waves and winds that blow
> How sweet to reach that shore,
> And bid farewell to life below
>   For evermore.

> There blessed will be my days
> Beyond both world and grave,
> With all eternity to praise
>   The peace he gave:
> The Lamb's high company
> With no more thought of sin,
> Will ever sing of Calvary
>   And I with them.

Thomas William, Bethesda'r Fro (1761-1844)

Another writer who knew the first leaders of the Revival and lived on into the 19th century was Thomas Williams. He was indebted for his upbringing in the faith to David Jones (1736-1810), Vicar of Llangan (Glamorgan) and strong supporter of the Methodist cause. Thomas William joined the Methodists and was for twenty years a hard worker for the cause. In the troubles of Peter Williams, the editor of the great annotated family Bible which appeared in 1770, Thomas William took his side. Peter Williams had early been accused of heresy but had received the firm support of the early Methodist leaders. But within a year of the death of William Williams, Pantycelyn in 1791 Peter Williams was again attacked and this time expelled, although he was now over seventy. In disgust Thomas William left the Methodists and founded a totally independent church of which he became the minister. This group eventually built a chapel and called it Bethesda. This became the name by which he is distinguished from so many others, and the name appears on his most important collection of hymns *Waters of Bethesda* (*Dyfroedd Bethesda* 1823). The title comes however from the first hymn in the collection:

'Rwyf finnau'n un o'r lliaws mawr'

I also, like so many more,
  Am here beside the pool;
Waiting the Holy Ghost to stir
  These waters deep and cool.

Within salvation's crystal flood,
  Through time's long ages proved,
How many hearts found health again
  And all disease removed!

Beside the pool for many a day
  My soul has been in grief;
And every hour is like a year,
  In waiting God's relief.

And shall it be that I must die,
  Who have remained so long?
Before me others always go
  And wash, and they are strong.

I was the first of all to come,
  But they were first made whole!
When shall the day of healing dawn
  On *my* unhappy soul?

Here shall I tarry, come what may,
  For who is there can tell
But the Physician will himself
  Come soon, and make me well?
                    (trans. H. Elvet Lewis)

This is unusual in that it is a meditation on a story from the Gospels. In its thoughts of death it expresses a theme important to the author, but its general spirit owes much to the general feeling of the period after the excitement and confidence of the early years of the Revival. It is difficult to imagine William Williams, Pantycelyn having such hesitations as are here expressed, sympathetic though they may be to a later generation. Thomas William was fine writer, as good as any of the Welsh hymn writers, and to it is unfortunate that there is this autumn chill over much of his work.

Edward Jones, Maes y Plwm (1761-1836)

Edward Jones was born in Denbighshire. After some neglect in his early years he managed to get a good education by his mid-twenties. He had been taken by his mother to hear the great Methodist preachers, but is was the reading of Bunyan's *Pilgrim's Progress* that brought him to conversion and to membership of the Methodist movement in 1787. He remained loyal for the rest of his life. In 1801 he went with his second wife and his numerous children (17 in all) to live in the farm house called *Maes y Plwm* (Lead Field).

He had a keen mind and deployed his interests widely — in farming, accountancy, schoolteaching, printing and as a Methodist elder. But running alongside this, as so often in Wales, he was a poet. He published a number of collections of hymns, carols and other verse. Unlike William Williams, Pantycelyn he was fully aware of the Welsh poetic traditions, and his carols are among the best of their kind. His hymns are without the storm and thunder, the depths and heights of the earlier writers: as Evan Isaac says, they sang their faith, he sang *about* his, in a period of great theological controversy. His preoccupation with the traditional metres and rime-schemes checks the spontaneity of his writing, as some of his contemporaries saw when they advised him to write in the freer forms. Nevertheless his hymns were useful in their day and some survive in the hymnbooks. The opening of this, the best known of his hymns, speaks more powerfully than any other in common use of the majesty of God:

'Mae'n llond y nefoedd, llond y byd'

He filleth heaven, he filleth earth,
  And hell too filleth he;
Eternal ages he doth fill,
  Unending Deity;
He filleth all earth's outer void,
His might is one, o'er all doth tower;
Boundless, almighty, endless being
  Source of all life and power.

111

Existing in himself, before,
  He framed the depth, the height,
Beyond the past eternal shore,
  He was the Infinite;
Without beginning of his days,
No end of life to him can be;
Eternal still in all his ways,
  The perfect Trinity.

(trans. v. 1 Miss Jane Owen
v. 2 H. Elvet Lewis)

Robert Williams (1766-1850)

Robert ap Gwilym Ddu o Eifion (Robert, son of Gwilym the Black of Eifion)

Robert Williams was a gangling giant of a man. He was brought up in comparatively wealthy circumstances in Eifion, that part of North Wales to the West of the great peaks of Snowdonia. Despite the shortage of educational opportunities in that area he was able to get a good education in both Welsh and English. He read widely; he played host to many of the poets of Wales at his farm. He shocked all who knew him and thought of him as a confirmed bachelor when at the age of fifty he married a quite young woman. He was happy in his marriage and his only child, a daughter, was the apple of his eye. Tragically she died when she was only seventeen years old. His lament on her death is one of the finest of its kind in the language.

Much of his poetry is fine and his name would be remembered without his hymns. But he was also a great hymn writer, unlike many fine poets. His hymns are more objective than those of William Williams, Pantycelyn, but that is not to say that he was without feeling. This can be seen in this his most famous hymn, which is still in regular use:

'Mae'r gwaed a redodd ar y groes'

The blood that flowed upon the cross
  Ages untold remember;
Eternity will not suffice
  Its priceless worth to ponder.

The choir on high, for evermore
  Adores the blessed Saviour;
Melodiously the harps acclaim
  His name above all other.

Worthy the Lamb for sinner slain;
  Sweet strains extol his passion;
O'er seraphim's entrancing cry
  Rings high the saints' ovation.

In ages countless as the sand
  Still will expand the anthem;
New marvels of his agony
  Eternally will blossom.

His sacrifice's wondrous worth
  No tongue on earth can utter;
Eternity is not too long,
  Still new the song for ever.
                    (trans. Miss Jane Owen)

Peter Jones (1775-1845)
Pedr Fardd (Peter the Poet)

Peter Jones was born in Dolbenmaen, Caernarvonshire, son of
a weaver who was also something of a local poet himself. It is clear
that Peter benefited greatly from his father's example in many
ways, not least in that he learned the craft of the poet from him.
He probably worked as a weaver with his father until he was about
twenty five, when he moved to Liverpool, where there was a
strong Welsh community. He may have worked as a clerk there.
Certainly when a day-school was opened, connected with the two
Welsh churches in Liverpool, he became its schoolmaster for a
short time. That he hated the work is clear from one of his poems.
He was however something of a teacher to the whole community,
who sought him out for his wide reading and wise judgement. But
above all he was in demand by those wished to improve their
poetical craftsmanship, for he was a master of the traditional
forms with their strict rules of rime and alliteration. He published
a great deal of poetry which is marked more by its skill than its
power to move. He becomes a quite different writer with his

hymns. In these he shows a strength and command that makes it possible to compare him with William Williams, Pantycelyn. Few other hymn writers can compare with him in the strong structure of his hymns. Often the hymns in the Welsh hymn books are taken stanza by stanza from different authors. Pedr Fardd defies such treatment. A number of his hymns are in regular use by all denominations: one of the finest is this, which sets the work of salvation in it's widest context of the whole creative work of God.

'Cyn llunio'r byd, cyn lledu'r nefoedd wen'

Far before time, beyond creation's dawn,
Before the sun and moon and stars were born,
Salvation's way for sinners lost, undone,
Was counselled forth by God the Three in One.

A store of grace unlimited was laid
In Jesus Christ before the seas were made;
And precious cov'nant mercies did abound
In floods of blessing all the world around.

The trumpet sounds the note of glad release
On Calvary, by God's atoning grace:
Glad hymns of praise in every tongue shall be
For Jesus' blood and death that set us free.
                    (trans. Edmund Tudor Owen)

David Charles (1762-1834)

Thomas Charles, the great second generation leader of the Methodists and founder of the Welsh Sunday School movement wrote few hymns, and those of little distinction. His younger brother David made a great contribution in that field. He was a serious-minded child, and was unfortunate in that the family were unable to give him the kind of education that his elder brother received. He was apprenticed as a rope-maker in Carmarthen and went to Bristol to finish his training. On returning to his home town he joined the Methodists and became an elder. He began to preach in 1808 and was ordained in 1811. He was well known as a preacher and became a considerable leader of the movement in South Wales, taking a prominent part in drawing up the movement's *Confession of Faith*.

At least two of his hymns are classics of their kind. This first is a prayer for the Spirit's presence with the pilgrim in the trials of life:

'O Iesu mawr, rho d'anian bur'

Grant Thy pure Spirit, Jesu hear!
To a frail soul in desert drear;
To strengthen him through trials sore,
On the bleak way to Canaan's shore.

Every pure grace Thy Church is given,
Whether on earth, or up in heaven,
Shall all at once my soul possess
If with Thy spirit Thou me bless.

At peace beside Thy feet I'll cling
Thy precious blood's sweet praises sing,
Endure the cross, the Jordan quell
Grant but Thy spirit in me dwell.
                                    (trans. Miss Jane Owen)

The second is in many parts of Wales so often sung at funerals that the service would seem incomplete without it:

'Mae ffrydiau 'ngorfoledd yn tarddu'

The source of my joy and my rapture
  Has sprung from the bright throne above;
For there my Lord Jesus ascended;
  And there intercedes through His love;
The blood that stern justice demanded,
  Was shed upon God's throne on high,
A pledge of divine grace and mercy,
  That we, the condemned, shall not die.

Away from earth's wild desert valley
  To paradise we shall ascend;
Our faint, weary soul in God's bosom
  Shall sweetly repose in the end.
While safe in our refuge eternal
  From sin and from sorrow and pain,

We'll feast upon love without ending,
The love of the Lamb that was slain.

One day from the fair hills of Salem
The long desert way we shall view;
The trials and turns of the journey
Sweet memories then will renew;
We'll gaze upon terror and tempest,
On death and the grave, from above,
While safe from their reach we are soaring
Enraptured with peace and with love.

(trans. Miss Jane Owen)

Evan Evans (1795-1855)
Ieuan Glan Geirionydd

Evan Evan's parents were among those who founded the Methodist movent in Trefriw, the village in the Conway Valley. He was educated there and then in the free school in Llanrwst. At first he worked on his parents' small farm. When his parents were forced from this by poverty he went at twenty one as schoolmaster across the river in Talybont. From there he moved to Chester. He was already beginning to be known as a poet in the eisteddfod movement, writing in the traditional metres. He came to the attention of some prominent churchmen who persuaded him, despite the fact that he was a Methodist elder, to offer himself for ordination in the Established Church. He was ordained in Chester in 1826 and licensed to take the Welsh services in St Martin's, Chester. Later the same year he added the curacy of Christleton to his charge. In 1843 he moved to Ince but ill health and a longing for home after the death of his wife brought him back for two years to Trefriw in 1852. In July 1854 he took up the curacy of the church in Rhyl but he died in January of the following year.

He won a number of prizes in *eisteddfodau* and published a great variety of poetry. Besides his hymns he published a number of tunes (see page 167). Some of his hymns are translations or adaptations from the English of Watts, Perronet and others. In his poetry he often wrote of the longing of the exile for home: in his hymns that sense of exile is translated into longing for the final rest in heaven. In his hymns he is one of the very few who were successful in using some of the techniques of the traditional

116

Welsh poetry. This makes translation even more difficult than usual.

'Mae'm rhedfa is y rhod'

My race beneath the sun
Is very nearly run;
Life fades away in sad decay,
Soon shall my day be done:
My fragile tent is sorely rent,
My strength is spent well-nigh;
The hour is near — I must appear
In doubt and fear within the clear
Immortal sphere on high.

Grant, Lord, Thy peace to me
And thy dear face to see;
Before my day has passed away,
All sinless may I be!
Thy gracious light in death's dark night
Shall soon my fright dispell:
In Thy right hand on yonder strand,
Where fears disband my soul shall stand
Sweet land! where all is well!

(trans. H. Elvet Lewis)

Despite all this craftsmanship in words which was being used in the service of the Revival, it has been said that there have been in Welsh only two hymn writers of the first class, none in the second class and that the rest are in the third and below. Many would dispute that statement but it is certain that there was only one equal in power to William Williams, Pantycelyn and that in worldly terms she was a strange candidate for that honour.

Ann Griffiths (1776-1805)

Ann was the daughter of John and Jane Thomas of the small farm of Dolwar Fach, to the north of Newtown in the central valley of Wales. Her parents were devout worshippers at the local parish church and regular in family prayers. Ann is said to have been frivolous in her ways when she was young. One by one the family were converted to Methodism and joined the Methodist

117

group at Pontrobert. The family prayers became an open meeting and the house a center for Methodism in the area, welcoming many traveling preachers.

Ann was only eighteen when her mother died and Ann took over the running of the house for her father and brother John. In 1804 Ann married Thomas Griffiths of Meifod who came to live in Dolwar Fach. In 1805 Ann gave birth to a daughter. The child lived only a fortnight; Ann died a fornight later, probably from a weak heart caused by recurring attacks of rheumatic fever in her youth.

Such in bald outline is her story. She did not travel far, probably never farther than over the hills to Bala. It is her spiritual pilgrimage that has put her among the great poets of Wales and indeed of Europe. As the Anglo-Welsh poet R.S Thomas writes in his fine *Fugue for Ann Griffiths*

> There are other pilgrimages
>   to make beside Jerusalem, Rome:
> beside the one into the no-man's-
>   land beyond the telescope's carry.

Ann's elder brother, John, was the first to find an answer to his spiritual longings by joining the Methodists who at that time worshipped in a nearby farmhouse. Gradually the whole family felt the influence of this religion of the heart, but Ann was not the kind of character that gave way easily. We have no portrait of her, except in the words of John Hughes, the minister who married Ruth Evans and who was a kind of spiritual confidant to Ann.

> As far as her appearance goes she was of delicate physique, her complexion fair and rosy, a quite high forehead, dark hair, taller in stature than is usual for a woman, smiling eyes above the curve of the cheek, and of a quite noble appearance, but despite that entirely easy to approach in the kind of fellowship that she enjoyed.

She was in her youth high spirited; 'wild' even 'flighty' would have been the words for her. She was said to have been mad on dancing. This probably means that she joined vigorously in the games and dancing that marked the parish church festivals — things much looked down upon by the Methodists. Ann in turn had looked down on the Methodists before she joined them, and indeed made fun of them. She had some schooling in her earlier years and even learnt to read and write English. But even with this small education, one must not think of her or her family as lacking in culture. The area was rich in the traditional culture and even today retains carol and ballad singing traditions lost elsewhere. The making of poetry was and is taken for granted in such a Welsh community, and Ann's father was said to have written carols. There would have been much singing of folk-songs at the dancing in Ann's youth. Even into this century such isolated farm houses as was Dolwar Fach have been centres of music making and of poetry, able to provide the material for a 'noson lawen' (happy evening) of song and poetry and story telling.

It is not known when Ann turned from the traditional form of Christianity in which she had been brought up to the more intense life of the Methodists. John Hughes tells us that she had an occasion to go to Llanfyllin and that there she met someone who had been a maid in the house and that through this encounter she went to an open air Congregational meeting. The Preacher was the Reverend Benjamin Jones of Pwllheli, well known as an author as well as for his preaching. In the course of the service Ann felt herself convicted of sin and resolved to turn her back on it. When she sought counsel from the vicar of the parish, he failed her. So she turned to the Methodists and through the ministry of the Reverend Israel Jones of Llandinam found that her sins were forgiven. She joined the chapel at Pontrobert sometime in 1797, a period of strong revival experience in that congregation. She turned also to Bala, the centre of Methodism in North Wales, to the ministry of Thomas Charles, and she and others would make the twenty mile journey there for the Communion Sunday, returning late from the service with singing and with prayer, even when there was snow on the ground.

Among her companions on these journeys was Ruth Evans, the maid at Dolwar. This was more than a mistress and maid relationship: Ruth and Ann enjoyed a deep spiritual fellowship, and because of it Ann's hymns have been preserved. Only one stanza in Ann's own handwriting survives, at the end of a letter. The rest have come down to us through the memory of Ruth Evans. Ann, it seems, would compose her verses and recite them to Ruth who would find a suitable tune for them. Ann put very few of them on paper. Ruth could not read or write, but as so often in such societies even today, her memory was good. In 1804 she married John Hughes and after Ann's death she dictated the hymns to her husband. Although the hymns suffered greatly at the hands of editors and improvers in the 19th century, the notebooks of John Hughes survive and it is possible to discover from them what Ruth gave to him. Such is the distinction and power of that material that we can be sure that it is not the work of John Hughes. It is perhaps fortunate that he himself wrote hymns so that we can see the huge difference between those and the hymns ascribed to Ann. What is difficult is to be sure how the 76 stanzas that he transcribed are to be grouped. Some editors say that there are 26 hymns, others 29. It has been suggested that Ann in reality would meditate on a particular theme over a period of weeks or months, and that the fruit of her prayer would be from time to time a stanza, and that therefore, though they can be grouped by their subject matter, they were not planned and composed as a whole hymns.

Whatever may be one's judgement on that question there can be no doubt of the hymns' spiritual and poetical power. Ann was grounded in the Bible and the Prayer Book. There are clear signs of her familiarity with the hymns of William Williams, Pantycelyn. We know that she heard sermons from some of the great preachers, in particular from Thomas Charles of Bala. We know too the importance in her life of the visits of John Hughes when he moved to Pontrobert, with whom she would discuss theology by the hour, and whose letters to her clearly planted the seeds from which some of the hymns grew. All these elements are fused in the crucible of her sheer genius and of her own experience of the grace of God in Christ, that experience which would lead her sometimes into hours in which she would be lost to the world — hours of adoring prayer whose fruit might be another hymn.

She was, as a child of her time and of the Revival, deeply conscious of her own sinfulness. Her letters, themselves great pieces of religious prose, speak often of her sense that she is falling away and backsliding. But in her hymns the overwhelming theme is that of wonder. Typical of her is:

'Rhyfedd, rhyfedd gan angylion'

Wondrous sight for men and angels!
  Wonders, wonders without end!
He who made, preserves, sustains us,
  He our ruler and our Friend,

Here lies cradled in the manger,
  Finds no resting-place on earth,
Yet the shining hosts of glory
  Throng to worship at his birth.

Her use of scripture is astonishing. In the next stanza she turns to the story of the people gathered at Sinai and forbidden to pass the barrier around the mountain; she uses this to express her sense of freedom in Christ:

When thick cloud lies over Sinai,
  And the trumpet's note rings high,
In Christ the Word I'll pass the barrier,
  Climb and feast, nor fear to die;
For in him all fullness dwelleth,
  Fulness to restore our loss;
He stood forth and made atonement
  Through his offering on the cross.
          (trans H.A.Hodges)

The next line is one that defies translation into verse

'He is the Propitiation that was between the
thieves'.

Ann's verses are full of such contrasts and contradictions, such as the hymn in which she meditates on the 'Way':

'Er mai cwbwl groes i natur'

Though altogether against nature
  Is the pathway which I tread;
Yet I'll brave it, and serenely
  'Neath the vision of thy face;
Take up the cross, a crown regard it,
  Despite oppression live serene;
This road is straight, though so entangled,
  And leads to the city of our peace.

A Way whose name is Wonderful,
  Old and yet for ever new,
Without beginning, yet not ageing,
  Whereon the dead their life renew;

A Way which can attract its travellers,
  A Way that's Husband, ay that's Head,
A Way made holy which I'll follow
  To rest therein beyond the veil.

Way by eye of kite unnoticed
  Though it shine as noonday sun;
It is hidden and untrodden
  Save for those with faith aglow;
A Way to justify the godless
  A Way to raise the dead to life,
A Way to bring God's peace to sinners,
  Justice being preserved the while.

A Way design'd e'er time began,
  Revealed to us to meet our need,
Through the promise made in Eden,
  Which first announced the woman's seed;
Here is based the second compact,
  By counsel of the Three in One,
Here is wine to bring refreshment,
  To cheer the heart of God and man.
          (trans. Robert O.F.Wynne
          and John Ryan)

It is unlikely that Ann ever saw the sea or indeed any greater stretch of water than the lake at Bala, but the imagery of water and of the sea is very strong — it is her symbol of the Godhead:

'O to spend my life in a sea of wonders'.

or

'To swim in the pure river of life, the endless peace of the Three in One'.

But it can also be the troubled way through life, as in the fourth verse of the next hymn — stanzas which seem to demand to be taken together since they are in an unusual metre for Ann. They begin with a highly typical uniting of ardent devotion with pure orthodox theology in the first two stanzas. The third expresses the longing that continually returns to be with God for ever. The necessities of translation demand otherwise but in the original the last word is 'God' as Ann indeed finds that the last word is with God: 'because the ark is God'.

O am gael ffydd i edrych

O might I gain faith's insight,
  With angel-minds on high,
Into Heaven's secret counsels,
  Its saving mystery;
Two natures in one Person
  Joined indivisibly,
True, pure and unconfounded,
  Perfect in unity.

Behold him all-sufficient,
  My soul, thy need to fill;
Take heart, and cast upon him
  The weight of every ill;
True man, in all thy weakness
  He truly feels for thee;
True God, o'er world, flesh, Satan
  He reigns victoriously.

Each day from the fierce conflict
  I long to turn aside —
Not leave the ark, or Israel,
  But turn from human pride,
And come to the King's table,
  who bids me go up higher,
When in the dust to love him
  Was all I durst desire.

Though strong may be the tempests
  And swellings of the sea,
Yet Wisdom is the pilot;
  A mighty Lord is he;
Though sin comes flooding round me,
  Its billows rising fast,
The ark is God almighty,
  And all is safe at last.
                    (trans. H.A.Hodges)

The last two lines of the third stanza bring forward another strong theme about which there has been much discussion. Is Ann a mystic? If so she is that near contradiction in terms, a Calvinistic mystic. Her longing for God is clearly at times over-whelming. But for her The Godhead is to be gazed upon, mar-velled at. As in the last hymn, the Incarnation is a mystery upon which the mind is stretched to the uttermost to understand, but her prayer is for insight into the mystery not to be united in mystical union with it. Following a long tradition (which proba-bly came to her through the hymns of William Williams, Pantycelyn as well as through her own reading of the Bible) she uses the imagery of the *Song of Songs* to express her love (or is it the love of the Church?) for the heavenly Bridegroom, as in these isolated four lines: 'Rhyfedd fyth, Briodas ferch'

> O wonder always, happy bride,
> To whom thou art in love allied,;
> Ye ransomed seed, his wonders tell,
> Who o'er ten thousand doth excel.

But 'alliance' is not to lose ones nature entirely in the godhead as the mystic desires. The greatest of her love songs to her saviour preserves that distinction. Here is a healthy love, not the hot-house eroticism of the cloister. There is no reason to believe that Ann's composing of hymns ended with her marriage: she was the same Ann while she was carrying the child that was to be the occasion of her early death.

> Wele'n sefyll rhwng y myrtwydd
>
> There he stands among the myrtles,
>   Worthiest object of my love;
> Yet in part I know his glory
>   Towers all earthly things above;
>   One glad morning
>   I shall see him as he is.
>
> He's the beauteous Rose of Sharon,
>   White and ruddy, fair to see;
> Excellent above ten thousand
>   Of the world's prime glories he.
>   Friend of sinners,
>   Here's their pilot on the deep.

What have I to do henceforward
  With vain idols of this earth?
Nothing can I find among them
  To compete with his high worth.
    Be my dwelling
  In his love through all my days.
          (trans. H.A.Hodges)

The words of the contemporary poet R.S.Thomas now may
have some meaning to the English reader:

Down this path she set off
for the earlier dancing
      of the body: but under the myrtle
the Bridegroom was waiting
      for her on her way home.

For all that one may marvel at Ann's intellect (R.S.Thomas
again:

Is there a scholarship that grows
naturally as the lichen? How
did she, a daughter of the land, come
by her learning?)

yet her chief glory is that she shares with us the intensity of her
own faith and love. If there is a reason for Welsh to be preserved,
for one who has not Welsh to learn the language, it could well be
the hymns of Ann Griffiths. So much of the poetry is lost in
translation, that it is best to leave the final word on Ann once
again to R.S.Thomas:

Here for a few years
the spirit sang on a bone bough
at eternity's window, the flesh trembling
at the splendour of a forgiveness
too impossible to believe in, yet believing.

The Present

If this were a book in Welsh for those who Sunday by Sunday
sing in that language it would be necessary to follow the course of

Welsh hymn writing through the 19th century so as to show the place of many of the well-known hymns and to give some account of their authors. For the purposes of this book that is not necessary. There is no history to retell either, as there is in England in particular, of the various movements in the church and how they affected the hymnody. Once the pattern had been set in the first generations the nature of a Welsh hymn was largely known.

There have been hymns brought in from other hymn singing cultures. There will be found in most Welsh hymn books translations of the great classics from German and from English. In the Established Church, which became The Church in Wales, the effects were felt of the movements in England that brought hymn singing into all its services in the course of the 19th century. The various hymn books for their use can clearly be seen to have been modelled on English books from *Hymns Ancient and Modern* onwards. *Emynau'r Eglwys* (*Hymns of the Church* words 1941, music 1951) is closely modelled on *English Hymnal* 1906 and contains many translations, almost a hundred from Latin, nearer two hundred from English, ten from German and five from Greek. With over six hundred hymns this does leave room for an extensive collection of Welsh hymns, but it does have a different emphasis from the books that are more specifically Welsh. Also for the Church in Wales is *Emynau Hen a Newydd* (1954 *Hymns Old and New*), with a much more Welsh feel to its contents.

The books of the various chapels are naturally yet more specifically Welsh, although they contain the classics from other hymn cultures. *Llyfr Emynau a Thonau* (1929 *The Book of Hymns and Tunes*) was prepared for the Calvinistic and Wesleyan Methodists. With 770 Welsh texts and 631 tunes it is the most comprehensive and representative collection of Welsh hymns in print; it also contains scripture passages for chanting and a small anthology of anthems. *Y Llawlyfr Moliant Newydd* (1956 *The New Handbook of Praise*) is the Baptists' book. It is smaller with 826 texts and 477 tunes and a smaller selection of scripture texts and anthems, but is handsomely produced and well edited. *Y Caniedydd* (1961 *The Songbook*) is the Congregationalists' hymnbook, with 920 texts and 501 tunes. Again there is a small collection of scripture texts and some anthems. All three of these books have a small collection of English texts without tunes. The most significant recent productions have been for the Sunday Schools and youth movements. *Mawl yr Ifanc* (1970 *Youth Praise*) is from the Baptists and *Caniedydd yr Ifanc* (1980 *The Youth Songbook*) is from the Congregationalists. Both are fairly dependant on translations from English, the Baptist book often giving the original alongside the Welsh. Neither book breaks new ground in Welsh hymn writing.

There were revival movements in the churches and chapels of the land throughout the 19th century and into the early years of this, some quite local, a few nation wide, and these have left their mark in the hymns that were written as in the buildings that often bear significant dates. But none of these changed the course of church life, and in more recent years there have been few stirrings of the Spirit of the old kind. There is a longing and much earnest prayer and exhortation, just as there was in the generation before the Great Revival in the 18th century, but in most places it takes much perseverance to remain steadfast and hopeful.

The present scene is dismal. In 1985 there was published a booklet for the celebration of the 250th anniversary of the conversion of Hywel Harris and the beginning of the Methodist Revival. The hymns are under three headings: 'The Eighteenth Century', with all the familiar names present; 'This century' with hymns written in recent decades, but largely in the old idiom; and 'The New Song', with twenty hymns which are almost without exception translations from English collections of worship songs of the charismatic movement. This is not to condemn the movement or its songs: it does make clear however the sad lack of anything in Welsh that remotely corresponds to the outburst of hymn writing that has been such a feature of the world of hymns in English. This does not mean that the Welsh hymn is dead. It does await a re-awakening.

Chapter 5

SINGING
THE WELSH HYMNS

The History of the Welsh Tunes
and the Congregational Singing
in Wales

Singing the Welsh Hymns

The history of the Welsh Tunes and of Congregational Singing in Wales

The achievements of the Welsh hymn writers have been great but it has proved difficult to export their work outside the circle of those who understand the language. Only one hymn text has broken the barrier to be present in virtually every hymn book in English, 'Guide me, O thou great Jehova/Redeemer'. The story of the Welsh hymn tunes is quite different. They now appear in every book in English and in books in a number of other languages.

The first to appear almost universally in books in the British Isles was Joseph Parry's ABERYSTWYTH. It began to circulate soon after it was composed and probably influenced the way people outside Wales have thought of the Welsh hymn tunes ever since. For the first thing that almost anyone will say about them is that they are powerful, mournful tunes in the minor key, which is a totally accurate description of ABERYSTWYTH, but of few others. If the subject is pursued and a list of the best-known Welsh tunes is drawn up (for example ST DENIO/JOANNA: RHUDDLAN: GWALCHMAI: CWM RHONDDA: ASH GROVE: AR HYD Y NOS/ALL THOUGH THE NIGHT: LLANFAIR: HYFRYDOL: RHOSYMEDRE: CRUGYBAR) it will be some time before the name of a tune in the minor key turns up (such as EBENEZER: BRYN CALFARIA: LLANGLOFFAN). It is true that they do have, be they major or minor, at their best a powerful rhetoric that is all their own. They have their own history too, that is quite separate from the way that church music was developing across the border in England.

The hymn tunes that are distinctive to Wales were written from the middle of the 18th century. For a century there followed a trickle of fine tunes. The full flowering did not come however until the second half of the nineteenth century. It is instructive to look at the earlier tunes, to see in them the roots of that later flowering. Among these tunes there are those that have not only done good service in Wales but have taken their place beyond the boundaries of the land and the use of the Welsh language.

At every step the history of the tunes will be found to be closely connected with what was happening to the way they were sung.

Those who worked to produce better tunes were equally concerned to see that the tunes were also sung better and that they proved a better contribution to the worship of their countrymen and women.

The Psalm tunes of Edmwnd Prys

The very first tunes to be published for use with Welsh words are the twelve printed with the *Salmau Can* of Edmwnd Prys which came out in 1621, making this the first provision of congregational material for the Welsh both in words and music. The meters that Prys developed differ from the common English meters as has already been seen, in particular the 'Welsh Psalm Meter' (8787 see page 88). He did not provide tunes that catered for this. His tunes are all in the English meters, and it must have been necessary to repeat the last note of the second and fourth lines to accommodate the words.

Edmwnd Prys gives no names for his tunes. Most of them are tunes well known in the English and Scottish books, under such names as MARTYRS, WINDSOR or DUNDEE, SOUTHWELL, OLD HUNDREDTH and OLD ll3th. ST MARY is not known before its appearance here, though that is no guarantee that it was not in circulation before Prys used it. Playford printed a version of it in 1677 and in that version it has been common in hymnbooks ever since, although its angular nature makes it suitable for only a restricted number of texts.

ST. MARY
Edmond Prys, *Psalter*, 1621

The mystery in the collection is the first tune, set to Psalm 1. It appeared two years later in Wither's *Hymns and Songs of the Church*, set to SONG 67, by which name the tune is usually known. The rest of the tunes in Wither's book are by the great English composer, Orlando Gibbons. Since Prys' book appeared in 1621 and Wither's in 1623, Gibbons must have taken an existing tune and provided it with a bass, something that he did nowhere else as far as we can tell in that collection. On the other hand Prys makes no attempt to match the tune with the Welsh Psalm Meter so that it is likely that he borrowed it also.

Melody and Bass
as given by Orlando Gibbons

SONG 67

It is possible that the psalm singing of the Established Church in Wales was enriched, at least in the places most within reach, by the developments in the editing and composing of tunes that were taking place in England at the end of the 17th century and the beginning of the 18th. There is however no record of that, and what is certain is that there was no further publication of tunes for the Welsh metrical psalms until 1770. In that year Ifan Williams the harpist who assisted Edward Jones in his publications of Welsh harp tunes, and a fine harpist himself produced twentyfour tunes which were printed at the end of a new edition of the *Book of Common Prayer* in Welsh. Ifan Williams took sixteen of them from English collections, giving them Welsh names, and composed the last eight himself. Here is an example of his work:

ST. BEUNO   from *Welsh Book of Common Prayer*, 1755

Ifan William

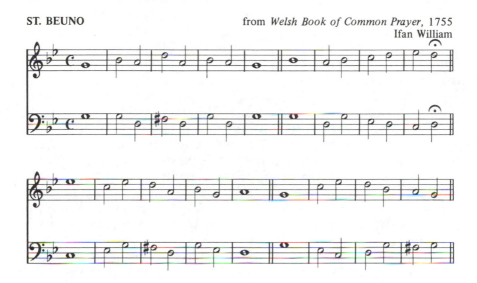

The tunes of the Revival

The lack of publications does not indicate a lack of interest in singing. Before the Revival began in 1734 there were those who were working to improve the standards of worship in the Established Church by improving the standard of the singing of the metrical psalms. The traveling singing teachers were the means by which this was achieved. Howell Harris refers to the work of a number of these in the Talgarth area, and it is clear that the singing meetings were from time to time an opportunity for him to pray and to preach and so to gain converts. Some of these teachers came into the Methodist movement, which, it must be remembered, was a movement within the Church of England, however much the church authorities looked down on it. Others remained with the traditional ways of the Church of England and there are clear records of singing teachers working in parishes and of parish bands of instruments through into the 19th century. The emphasis however was not on congregational singing, as the work of John Williams (1740-1821, Ioan Rhagfyr) of Celynnin in Meirionethshire makes clear. He learned the trade of hat maker from his father. By the standards of his times he had some education; he showed musical ability on flute and trumpet. He ran musical classes up and down North Wales and taught the elements of music to many of the poets and musicians of the next generation. But his chief contribution was as a church musician. He wrote many tunes and anthems, and this shows to what extent the parts of the Church not affected by Methodism placed the emphasis still on the choral parts of the worship rather than on the congregational singing.

On the whole the leaders of the singing in the parishes were men of less education than John Williams, modest though his education was by modern standards. Many of those whose name we know held the humble office of *clochydd* in the parish, that is they rang the church bell and acted as sexton, digging graves. It seems to have been common for them to show an interest in the music of the parish and to hold classes, presumably to teach tunes. There was as yet no book in Welsh on the elements of music for them to use, and some of the teachers must have known little more than their pupils. Some of them seem to have been sceptical of those who claimed to be able to decipher a tune from the marks on a page. In any case the singing was in unison, as it was to remain for many years.

Some of these early musicians had a wider influence, and none more than Dafydd Siencyn Morgan (David Jenkin Morgan 1752-1844). He was the son of a *clochydd* who was himself well known as a singer and musician at Llangrannog, Cardiganshire. Dafydd had his first lessons in music from his father, but did not inherit his father's fine voice. Little of his early life is known. It is said that he joined the militia at Pembroke Dock and that he played in the band, learning the clarinet. On his return from service he continued his musical studies with the English grammar of music by Tansur. He was appointed leader of the singing in the parish church, and he began to conduct singing classes. His fame spread and invitations came first from within his own county and then from farther afield. He made several journeys, stopping in various centres to conduct classes, travelling as far as Anglesey in North Wales and to the South Wales industrial valleys. Because of this he had to give up his office in the parish church and he moved to live in Llechryd in the same county, where he joined the Congregational Chapel and was appointed to lead the singing. He did not however confine his services to one denomination. It is said that he did most of his work in the parish churches since the best voices were there at that time. Certainly the musical tradition was better established there. He taught people the elements of music and taught them to sing in a more orderly fashion. There were no books of tunes published in Welsh nor books of instruction, and there was much copying by hand and even more teaching by ear. It is not known when Dafydd Siencyn Morgan began to compose, but in 1824 he won a competition in Welshpool with a hymntune, and shortly after that his hymntunes began to appear in the periodicals. There are tunes by him in Richard Mills *Caniadau Seion* (1840 *Songs of Sion,* see page 174) His tune MERCURIAL in that collection is really a small glee, and survives as an anthem, much developed by D. Emlyn Evans, under the title 'Teyrnasa Iesu Mawr' (Reign Great Jesus) in the current Congregational hymn book *Y Caniedydd* (1961). Only one survives as a hymntune in current books, PENLLYN, and it is difficult to disentangle its history. It appears in duple and triple time; in its early appearances it is in the major, it now always appears in the minor. As with all the tunes of this period the harmony has had to be rewritten because of the weaknesses in the original. This is however how a great pioneer of Welsh hymn singing is represented in the present day books.

PENLLYN.   David Jenkin Morgan

There was therefore a general increase of interest in the music of the Church's worship in the 18th century which began before the Methodist Revival. As that Revival developed it both encouraged singing in general and drew a number of the teachers of singing into the movement. One such was Henry Mills, (1757-1820) of Llanidloes, who came to the attenton of Thomas Charles of Bala who had him made official music director in the area. Through his work and that of his numerous descendants Llanidloes became for a period one of the most important centres for music in Wales.

The tunes of William Williams, Pantycelyn

Thus it was not in an entirely unmusical church and certainly not in an unmusical land that the Methodist movement was born and came to maturity with the publication of the hymns of William Williams, Pantycelyn. But what tunes did those first congregations sing? There were two sources in Wales to which Williams could look for tunes. The first, of course, was the metrical psalter of Edmwnd Prys which the traveling singing teachers used. Only four meters were given there of which Williams used three (Long Meter, Six eights and the Welsh Psalm Meter) and Williams clearly wished to expand into a much larger and more varied repertoire. The other native repertoire was that of the folk songs and the melodies that were used for the carols and ballads. These were readily available, in the sense that there were not wedded to any one set of words and it is surprising that Williams made so little use of them. It is only in one collection *Caniadau Duwiol* 1757 that he made any exception. There he used four, 'Nutmeg and Ginger', 'King's Farewell', 'Lovely Peggy', and 'Gwel yr Adeilad (See the building)'. The English names to these suggest that, like a number of tunes of this kind whose origin can be traced, they have an English origin. What is certain is that they had a wide circulation at that time in Wales and had become naturalized. Equally clear is that only one of these meters came into Welsh hymnody, that is 'Lovely Peggy' (8.8.8.6.D).

LOVELY PEGGY

Williams' example and influence in this may explain why no later generation has explored this quite large repertoire. Only LLANTRISANT, a rather dull, duple time version of the 'Awn i Fethlem' tune and TWRGWYN are to be found in present books. The latter is found in both major and minor, and is a noble melody though in the rather difficult 'Mentra Gwen' meter (see page 35), with its intriguing similarity in meter to the American 'Wondrous Love'.

TWRGWYN.

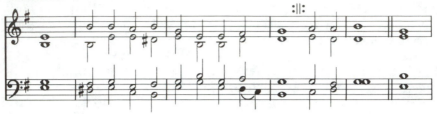

One further question arises before the Welsh origin of Pantycelyn's tunes and meters can be left. The meter 87.87.67 does not appear in English before the time of Williams. It is clearly related to the more familiar 87.87.47., which is of English origin, where the line of four syllables is usually repeated so that the tune can be 87.87.87. That meter is familiar in Latin hymns (e.g. Pange lingua gloriosi). Both it and 87.87.67. appear in the German hymns (e.g. 'Meine Hoffnung' by Neander). It is possible that Williams developed 87.87.67. from the 87.87.47. metre. It must be significant however that the words of his first hymn in the meter begin 'Dewch i'r frwydr' (Come to the battle), which are the first words of the Welsh War Song that Edward Jones (Bardd y Brenin) published in the second edition (1805) of *Musical and Poetical Relicks of the Welsh Bards*. If this is indeed an old song then here is a Welsh tune that Williams used to create a meter that became well used, even though the tune itself dropped out of use in Wales and has only recently been re-introduced. In the meantime it had been discovered by the English and after its inclusion in *English Hymnal* (1906), widely sung under the name RHUDDLAN. Here is the Welsh form:

RHUDDLAN

For the rest of his meters Williams turned to English sources, and from them also took the tunes to which his hymns were at first sung. But of course in introducing the new meters he opened both new influences in music and new possibilities for Welsh composers. He made possible the eventual flowering of the Welsh hymn tune.

The Tunes from 18th century sources

By the beginning of the 19th century congregational singing in Wales was attracting a good deal of criticism. There were still the old complaints that the congregations shouted their heads off, that they repeated the same verses and the same words over and over again; there was the swaying and leaping and jumping; there are references to the nodding of heads (presumably to keep time), to a drawling style of singing, with the hand held against the ear (a way of hearing one's own voice more clearly than one's neighbour's). In general this was singing that had little joy in it, though it was clearly the result of deep emotion. Besides these complaints, which went back to the early days of Methodist hymn singing, there were complaints about the triviality of the music that was being sung and its musical illiteracy. This coincided with the same kind of singing in England and was probably connected with it. Neverthless this period, of the last forty years of the 18th century and the first years of the 19th, saw the appearance of a number of the finest Welsh hymn tunes. No names of composers can be attached to these outstanding tunes, and there are often arguments about whether they are genuinely Welsh in origin. What is amply clear is that they became part of the genuine Welsh repertoire and that they became the standard for the development of Welsh hymn tunes. Dating these tunes is a mystery. They were published in a random kind of way in the first half of the 19th century, and it is quite obvious that the date of publication says little about the age of the tune or which was written before the other.

Some of the early tunes have clear links with the carol and ballad melodies, a number of which can be traced to the English stage of the early 18th century and to the broadside ballads of about the same time. Among the early hymn tunes there is a small group that have the same possible origins. It is worth giving or at least referring to all the tunes that can definitely be referred to

18th century sources. Throughout the following pages the names
of tunes will be translated where this is possible; if no translation
is given then the word is the name of a person or place.

SALOME has similarities with the Scottish tune TWEEDSIDE
that appears in John Gay's Ballad Opera 'Polly' of 1729. It may
have come to Wales direct from Scotland: again it may have been
brought by the cattle drovers from the streets and theatres of
London.

SALOME

(The tune appeared in this form in the mid-19 century books,
but today lacks the 'high kick' at the beginning of line 7, though
in other respects it remains the same).

The tune CAERLLEON has a similar history. It appeared in the
opera 'Flora' in 1729, and, with SALOME, in the 'Cobblers' Opera'
of the same year. In 1733 it turned up again in 'Achilles'. The

most ususal title in English was 'Come open the door sweet Betty'. It is not impossible that it originated in Wales, but the general indications would favour a borrowing from England.

CAERLLEON

Arranged: David Evans

CLOD (Praise) is a much more popular tune in Welsh use and beyond (often under the name FFIGYSBREN, Fig Tree). A tune very similar to this is in the 'Cobblers' Opera' of 1729 where it has the title 'The Fashionable Lady'. It also appears later as 'Death and the Lady' (*Old English Popular Music* William Chappell 1893). Again the argument has raged about whether it is English or Welsh in origin.

CLOD

The case of CYFAMOD (Covenant) is more complicated. Its origin can be traced to John Gay's 'The Beggar's Opera', the first and most famous of the Ballad Operas. There the title of the tune is given as 'Grim King of the Ghosts' (which appears to be a song that has been lost) and it is sung to the words 'Can love be controlled by advice?'. Under this title a similar melody appears in John Parry's *A Collection of Welsh, English and Scotch Airs* of 1761. Jane Williams, Aberpergwm, in her famous collection of folk songs from Glamorgan gives another clearly related melody set to the words 'Pan oeddwn ar ddydd yn cyd-rhodio' (As I was out walking one day). Meanwhile it had also become widely known, in a number of variants, as a carol/ballad melody under the name YR HEN DDARBI (The Old Darby). One of these, from a manuscript in the University Library, Bangor is now in use with English words. All these variants of the melody were in a 3/4 rhythm. Now came a totally Welsh development. The language tends to have an accent on the penultimate syllable of a word and for this to be a short syllable. This produces a tendency, to be seen often in the manuscript sources of Welsh tunes, for the next syllable to be extended; in this case the third note also has been extended and this has produced the extraordinary phenomenon of a tune in 5/4, except for the third phrase which remains in a simple triple rhythm. This 5/4 rhythm has to be understood in a quite special way. It is not to be sung in strict time (as if it were the movement *Mars* from Gustav Holst's *The Planets*) but allowing the words first to force the movement on from the first beat of the bar and then to drag out the second and third. The examples show three stages of development. The carol variant could have been chosen to give one more closely related to CYFAMOD, but the English carol written for this variant is interesting in its own right.

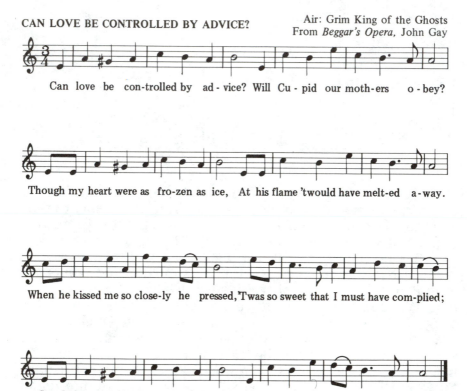

HOW DARK WAS THE NIGHT OF HIS COMING

Mesur: Yr Hen Ddarbi/Old Derby
Words: F. Pratt Green

Melody: arranged Alan Luff

1. How dark was the night of his coming!
   How bleak was the wind on the hill!
   How many, who slept till cock-crowing,
   had little to wake for but ill!
   Good shepherds, who stare into heaven,
   what see you so fair and so rare?
   What glory transfigures your faces?
   What songs are enchanting the air?

2. Those dutiful shepherds saw angels
   where most of us only see night;
   their beautiful vision escapes us
   who cease to believe in the light.
   The song is tossed back into darkness
   by winds that are bitter with hate;
   but shepherds have found in a manger
   that Saviour the ages await.

3. You angels, we see you, we hear you!
   We stand with our backs to the wind!
   The longer we listen, the stronger
   your message of hope for mankind.
   You sceptics and cynics, forgive us
   for leaving you out in the cold;
   we'll come back with songs of salvation,
   good news that shall never grow old.

CYFAMOD (Hen Ddarbi).

*Note: in some earlier Welsh hymn books the rhythm of the first and similar measures is notated

The tune RHAD RAS (Free Grace), which is called DIFYRRWCH GWYR TREFALDWYN (The delight of the men of Trefaldwyn) in some collections may have a similar origin. The name tempts one to set it alongside the many carol/ballad melodies that are given names beginning with *Difyrrwch* (Delight), and the melody has a number of parallels.

From the same period are the two tunes MORIAH and GWALIA which are so similar as to make it seem either that they are adapted one from the other, without it being possible to say which came first, or that they are both adapted from the same original. They both appear for the first time in collections of 1769 edited by Martin Madan, a barrister converted by John Wesley's preaching who became ordained and served as chaplain to the Lock Hospital, a Refuge for Foundlings. GWALIA was in the *Lock Hospital Collection* and MORIAH in Madan's *Collection of Psalm and Hymn Tunes*. Again it is quite impossible to say whether its origin was Welsh. At that time tunes were travelling from England to Wales both into the carol/ballad tradition and to be sung to the hymns of William Williams, Pantycelyn, and of those others who took over the new meters he developed. Florid tunes of this kind were being written in England. Yet on the other hand, why should Madan have used the name GWALIA if there were not a Welsh connection? At any rate the Welsh adopted the tunes and they appear in most Welsh collections of tunes.

GWALIA

147

MORIAH

The tune RHYDDID (Freedom) was ascribed to various composers in the early 19th century books, but the late 19th century musician Eos Llechyd recorded that he had seen the tune in a music note book which bore the name of John Jones, Caerludd (1725?-96) who was appointed one of the two organists of the Middle Temple in London in 1749, organist of the Charterhouse in 1753 and of St Paul's Cathedral from 1755, holding all these posts together. He was a colleague in these posts of many of the great names in music of the period. He published a number of works including a collection of psalm chants, but there seems to be no other published hymntune by him — or as he would certainly have referred to it psalm-tune.

RHYDDID

Two tunes still in use are ascribed to John Jeffries (1718?-98), though these were not published until the 19th century. DYFRDWY is in the Welsh Psalm Meter and thus has not attracted the attention it deserves. LLANGOEDMOR appears in a number of non-Welsh books, and in fact was the inspiration for a fine hymn by G.K.A. Bell (now often sung in three line verses to GELOBT SEI GOTT). The tune, with its bold leaps has made some liken it to the ringing of bells; this gave rise to the second half of verse one:

> Christ is the King! O friends, rejoice;
> Brothers and sisters with one voice
> Make all men know He is your choice.
> Ring out ye bells, give tongue, give tongue;
> Let your most merry peal be rung,
> While our exultant song is sung.

The tune receives a wide variety of treatment in present hymn-books, from a heavy fourpart harmony throughout to lighter textures using unison passages. It is interesting to compare these with the version given in Richard Mills' *Caniadau Seion* 1840: here there is more movement in the tune, and in the third line it stretches boldly up to a higher note than in any of the current versions.

LLANGOEDMOR

To complete the list of tunes that first appeared before 1800, or for which there is documentary evidence before that date, the problem of ARFON must be discussed. It appears in Edward Jones' *Relicks of the Welsh Bards* 1784, and came into some late 19th century Welsh books and from them into English books from *English Hymnal* 1906 onwards. It is very well known however as a French *Noel* to the words 'Joseph est bien marié'. A variant of it is used by Marc Antoine Charpentier (1637?-1704) as the melody on which he bases the *Kyrie* of his *Messe de Minuit*.

The tunes of probable 18th century origin

There are a number of other tunes whose origins are uncertain and are likely to have been contemporary with the tunes just discussed, though we have no direct evidence for that. They appeared in a number of collections in the first half of the 19th century, and the order of their appearance gives no indication of their order of composition. Only the tunes that have proved of interest outside Wales or that might prove to be of interest are given.

BRAINT (Privilege) certainly has an antique feel to it, being in the Dorian mode, unlike the great bulk of the Welsh tunes which are firmly in the modern major or minor. This puts it alongside many of the genuine Welsh folksongs and would indicate a considerable age. The meter however is is a strange one, probably invented by William Williams, Pantycelyn, possibly taking from a folksong the idea of the two strong syllables at the beginning that are its distinctive feature. As has been seen it was not his practice to borrow folk songs as such for use as hymn tunes, or one might suggest that this is such a direct borrowing. The name BRAINT comes from its connection with a late 18th century hymn which has 'Braint, braint' as its opening words, so that the name gives no assistance in tracing its origin. (The hymn has been translated as

O blest
Communion with the saints at rest!)

The tune is also known in Wales as TRAWSFYNNYDD, which is simply a place-name in North Wales. It has fascinated more than one contemporary Welsh composer and has been used in their works.

BRAINT

DINIWEIDRWYDD (Innocence) is a tune that deserves to be more widely known for its worshipful quality, although the feminine endings to all the odd numbered lines create problems in English. There is some evidence that it was sung in the ballad tradition to words by a poet who died in 1785. (Evan Powell, Llanfrynach). In the collections of the mid 19th century it is most often found in common time, but Ieuan Gwyllt has it a second time in the appendix to his *Llyfr Tonau Cynulleidfaol* 1859 in triple time, as it is most frequently sung today. As with many of the early Welsh melodies it is in a simple form in which the first two lines are repeated, as lines three and four, a new strain of melody introduced for lines five and six, and an exact return made to the first two lines for lines seven and eight (AABA). It shows a distinctive trick of these tunes that the lie of the melody, its tessitura, is quite different in the B section.

DINIWEIDRWYDD

A number of the oldest tunes appear (as did DINIWEIDRWYDD) in the very important collection *Caniadaeth y Cysegr* (1839 *Songs of the Sanctuary*) edited by John Roberts, Henllan (1807-76). Many of those in this collection must have been written in the early enthusiasm of the Revival. As a musician John Roberts was for the most part self-taught. He took down the tunes largely from two leaders of the singing in his area, Moses Parry, of Denbigh and John Peters who had led the singing in Henllan for almost half a centry. Two have become well known outside Wales.

JOANNA (as it is known in Wales, ST DENIO outside Wales) is the best known of them since its introduction in *English Hymnal* 1906 where it was first set to the words 'Immortal, invisible, God only wise', an association that has since gone everywhere that hymns are sung in English. It has a consiberable resemblance to the ballad entitled 'Can mlynedd i nawr' (A hundred years from now) which was popular in the early years of the 19th century, and of which a secular version appeared in the Kerry Manuscript, the collection of tunes made by by John Jenkins (Ifor Ceri 1770-1829), as 'Can mlynedd yn ôl' (A hundred years ago). As will be seen, many of the Welsh tunes in the major make great use of the notes of the major chord based on the keynote of the tune. This tune begins as though in a different key and only reaches the notes of the home key at the end of the first line. This thrusts into prominence the fifth note of the tune which signals that the first expectation is wrong. Without recognizing the technical reason the singer appreciates the additional impetus that this gives to the tune — a quality that has justly made it popular, though the words with which it is associated now begin to look somewhat tired and dated.

ST. DENIO

LLEDROD (also known as LLANGOLLEN) is in many ways akin to LLANGOEDMOR in the way it ranges widely up and down the major triad. It is a much more tightly constructed tune than the other with a strong sense of growth and an exuberance that is especially marked in the third line. It is probably of 18th century origin. It has been fairly widely used in non-Welsh books but has not been convincingly married yet to a text that has met wide favour.

LLEDROD

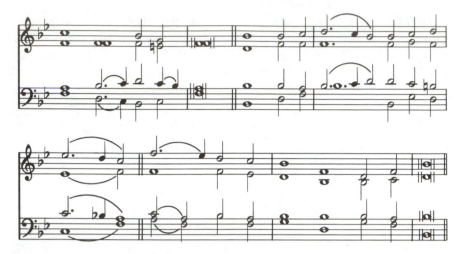

Of quite unknown origin is EDINBURGH which first appeared in *Caniadau Seion* (1840 edited by Richard Mills). It is difficult to see why this, with its engaging simplicity, has not traveled more widely.

EDINBURGH

CRUGYBAR is an important tune in the Welsh repertoire and has gained wide use in non-Welsh books. It is the tune that now belongs inescapably to the funeral hymn by David Charles 'The source of my joy and my rapture' (page 115). It origin has been much discussed. There are undoubted similarities in a number of early tunes, in the folk-song 'Y Fwyalchen' (The Blackbird), and the hymn tunes BETHEL and SALOME. At its first publication in 1883 in *Moliant Seion* the editor Cledan Williams added a note linking the tune with one of the most colourful women of the turn of the century, Nancy Crug-y-bar (Nancy Jones 1760-1833), tales of whose religious fervour were many and of her leading the singing in periods of revival. The evidence for this link however is minimal. In the 1890's there was a good deal of controversy over the origin of the tune, with Cledan Williams claiming that although it was founded on an old tune, most of the work was his. Over a number of years a number of possible originals were quoted, including a manuscript of 1809. In a recent article Rhidian Griffiths has summarized the arguments and concludes that its origin is in an old tune in triple rhythm that has suffered the common fate of Welsh tunes of having the original rhythm distorted by slow singing with heavy accentuation of the second beat of the bar (compare CYFAMOD). Cledan Williams probably did indeed give the tune that shape that made it almost immediately a popular success all over Wales.

CRUGYBAR

Although there are a number of other tunes in this class of those which may belong to the 18th century but cannot be placed accurately, and which appeared for the first time in print in the first half of the 19th century, they have not proved attractive outside Wales and need not be dealt with in detail. One other does deserve mention however. Y DELYN AUR (The Golden Harp) is a florid tune of the kind that often came under condemnation by the middle of the 19th century. In fact the first reference to it is of such a kind: Canon Thomas Jones in his *Welsh Church Tune and Chant Book* of 1859 rejects tunes of a 'trashy character' and specifically refers to Y DELYN AUR, proving its popularity at that time. It does not appear in print however until 1879. It is certainly a florid tune, as were many of those sung in the earlier years of the century, but it has a grandeur that most of them lack. As with many of the tunes in the 87.87.4.7. metre there are repetitions, the fifth line being repeated twice and the sixth three times. The tune is unusual in that it is all within the compass of a fifth and has no repetitions but relies on a steady growth from a number of small melodic elements. If it has a weakness it is that it spends too much time on the top note of the tune.

Y DELYN AUR *

Arranged: E. Stephen

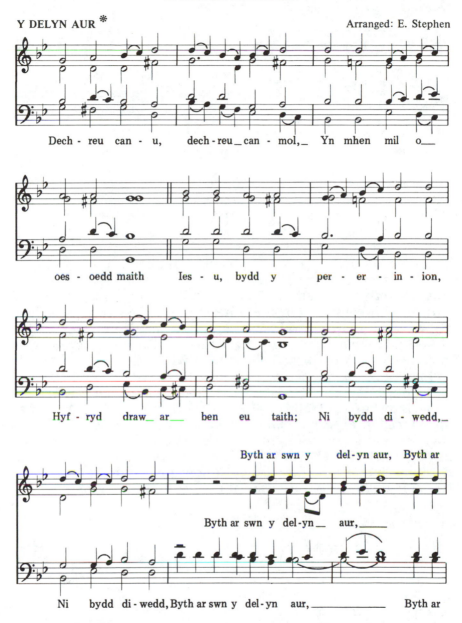

Dech - reu can - u, dech - reu _ can - mol, _ Yn mhen mil o _

oes - oedd maith Ies - u, bydd y per - er - in - ion,

Hyf - ryd draw _ ar _ ben eu taith; Ni bydd di - wedd, _

Byth ar swn y del - yn aur, Byth ar

Byth ar swn y del - yn _ aur, _____

Ni bydd di - wedd, Byth ar swn y del - yn aur, _____ Byth ar

swn y del-yn aur,   Byth__ ar__ swn__ y__ del - yn aur.

*Note: in later books it is usually arranged so that all voices sing throughout.

The first apearance that can be traced of LLANGLOFFAN is in *Llwybrau Moliant* (The Paths of Praise, Wrexham 1872). This was a collection for the use of Baptists edited by Lewis Jones of Treherbert. The tune is there harmonized by David Lewis who, with his father, were well known for their collecting and arranging of old Welsh tunes. A resemblance has been claimed between this tune and the English folk-song 'The Jolly Miller of Dee'. This may mean that it was transported from England into Wales in the 18th or 19th century. On the other hand it lives equally well in minor and major mode (in which it is sometimes called LLANFYLLIN) and this is a characteristic of the native Welsh folk melodies which perplexed those who wrote them down by the ambiguity of their tonality. This tune has done considerable service outside Wales. It follows the slightly unusual pattern for these early tunes of ABCB (although B develops from A). It was introduced in *English Hymnal* 1906 and the version there is probably by Vaughan Williams. It emphasizes the minor mode throughout. In David Lewis' version given here, and in the Welsh versions since then that closely follow his, there is a typically Welsh burst of major harmony at the beginning of line five.

LLANGLOFFAN

These then are the tunes that probably carried the singing of the first generations of the Revival, some having been borrowed and some having been created in that period. The character of the Welsh hymn tune begins to be seen in them. Apart from BRAINT they are very much of their period, being strongly in the major or minor mode as was all the popular composing of the period, following the examples of the great masters who were active in London. The tunes in the major tend to make considerable use of the notes of the main triads of the key, but this always has been a strong way to construct a tune.

The church musicians of the early 19th century

These important early tunes were being published at the beginning of the 19th century precisely because there were a number of good musicians active in Wales at that time. Some of them had purely local influence: some published books of tunes. A number of them have left us the occasional useful tune, very much in the style of those that they inherited from the generation before. They were working however under great disadvantages. None of them were professional musicians and this led, particularly in the early part of this period, to their work being important only in a small area of influence. Their tunes were often full of mistakes in the harmony, and have needed the hand of later editors to make them usable today.

The fundamental problem of the period following the Revival was precisely that there was no musical education available in Wales. Many of the traveling Psalm teachers were ignorant of music and simply taught by rote. As has happened so often, an existing situation was taken to be the will of God and elevated to a commandment, and thus many religious leaders condemned singing from notation as ungodly. The singing was in unison and without instrumental support. William Williams, Pantycelyn, had objected to the use of instruments and that tradition prevailed, with many of the religious leaders of the time suspicious of any development. They were content with the old tunes, bad as well as good, and with the old ways of singing them.

It was in 1797 that John Williams (Sion Singer 1750-1807) published the first book in Welsh on the elements of music, *Cyfaill mewn llogell* (*A Friend in the pocket*). The book is in the form of a dialogue between Orpheus, the teacher, and Indoctus, the pupil. This however does nothing to make the book easy to understand. In places it is quite misleading. Even the Welsh translation of 'The Scale of Music' which he gives in the book's subtitle is wrong since he uses the word *Clorian* which means the kind of scale on which things are weighed. Nevertheless here was for the first time an explanation of musical notation in Welsh, and this part of the book was reprinted in 1811 as the appendix to a book of hymns.

It was not until 1817 that a satisfactory book on the elements of music was published. This was a translation of a handbook by Charles Dibdin. It was the work of Owen Williams (1774-sometime after 1827) who went on to publish in the next year a book on the principles of singing. At the end of the year the two works were published in one volume and this *Gamut* was of the greatest of value in its day and must have been in the possession of every musician in the land. Owen Williams continued his usefulness to the singing of the churches by publishing in 1819 two books of tunes under the title of *Brenhinol Ganiadau Sion* (*The Royal Songs of Sion*), the first in the meters found in the metrical psalms of Edmwnd Prys and the second of tunes in the new meters introduced by William Williams, Pantycelyn. He somehow gained the help of Samuel Wesley and Vincent Novello, two of the leading English musicians of his day, in both writing and arranging tunes, which were printed on two staves, an innovation in Wales at that time and a considerable step forward. One source of regret about his collections of tunes is that, although he names a number of composers in his introduction, he does not put their names to the tunes. One tune whose composer has been traced and which is widely known is BRYNHYFRYD by John Williams (1740-1821) of Dolgellau, first a hat-maker, following his father, and then a solicitor's clerk, and then a schoolmaster. He was one of the best known musicians of his time, and among his other tunes are SABATH, CEMAES and DYFROEDD SILOAH (The Waters of Siloah).

BRYNHYFRYD

At about the same time another musician was collecting, editing and writing tunes, John Ellis of Llanrwst (1760-1839). His own tunes and anthems show a gift for writing melodies but they are full of weaknesses and mistakes when he comes to composing harmony. In 1816 he published *Mawl yr Arglwydd* (*The Lord's Praise*). The last tune he composed was ELIOT, which still survives in all the Welsh hymn books, and which could well be useful to English words.

ELIOT

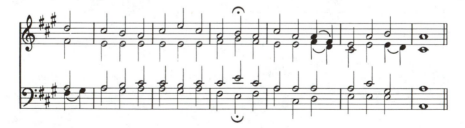

Books on music and collections of tunes now began to appear in a steady, if not great flow. John Harris (1802-23) published *Grisiau Cerdd Arwest* (*Steps in Music*) at the end of his short life, a book of only twenty pages, but with the elements of music so clearly explained that it gained a wide circulation.

Not all the books were good ones. William Owen (1788-1838), a schoolteacher, brought out his book *Y Caniedydd Crefyddol* (*The Sacred Songbook*) in 1828, with his own lessons on the principles of music, essays on music by a variety of writers and a collection of tunes. The lessons are obscure and full of mistakes: among the tunes are some of the very weak material that was at that time being brought into Wales, feeble melodies over repetitive harmonies, decked out with runs, repetitions of words and the kind of entries for individual voices that give them the name 'fuguing tunes'.

The Reverend J.D.Edwards (1805-85) graduated from Jesus College, Oxford in 1830 and after serving curacies he became in 1843 Rector of Rhosymedre near Wrexham. In 1836 he published the first collection of music for the established church in Wales, *Original Sacred Music*, it being his desire to have all the congregation sing. He brought out a second volume in 1843. His best and most popular tune is called either LOVELY or by the name of the parish he served, RHOSYMEDRE.

RHOSYMEDRE

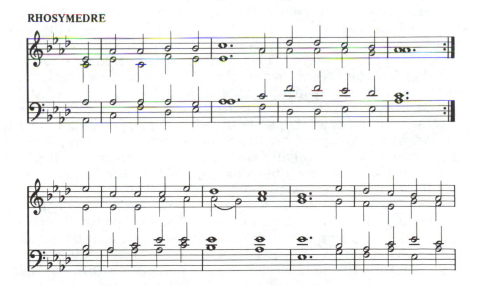

Alongside these early publications there was growing a strong movement of Schools of Singing and Musical Societies. These were founded to teach Christians to sing as part of their worship, but they were not for the most part denominational. The first recorded school was in Carneddi Chapel, Llanllechid, Bethesda, in North Wales, and was taught by Robert Williams (1790-1828). He began in 1819 to teach music to children and young people on Saturday afternoons: at six o'clock the adults would gather to learn the tunes to be sung in the Sunday services. His work became famous and people travelled long distances to hear the singing. He died as a result of an accident in the slate quarry where he worked, but soon after his death his pupils joined together to found the 'Society of Christian Singers of Carneddi Chapel'. They drew up a list of rules that make interesting reading today. They set out the government of the Society and the arrangements for the meetings, but they also set out the Christian standards that were expected of members. Rule 12 makes it quite clear that the Society will have nothing to do with musical instruments; they are described as dead things; only the human voice serves the praises of God. These rules set a pattern for the many societies that grew up all over Wales in the succeeding years and in which were raised many of the influential musicians of the period. They contributed greatly to the unity of music in Wales because their doors were open to Christians of all persuasions at a time of great development in music and singing. By the middle of the century the denominations were producing their own books of hymns and their own tune-books, but by then the foundations had been laid of a general hymn culture in the land.

Alongside the Singing Societies there grew up the Temperance Choirs, beginning with the founding of the first Welsh Temperance Society in Liverpool in 1835. The movement spread quickly and in 1836 there was the first Temperance Festival in Wrexham. A great feature of the festivals were the processions through the streets with the singing of Temperance songs. These tunes began to feature in the collections of hymn tunes, but by 1840 the first enthusiasm had begun to flag and criticisms began to be heard about the poor quality of the songs and their tunes. Attempts were made after a revival of the movement in 1850 to improve the quality of the songs, since it was recognized that they were having a bad effect on the hymn singing in the churches.

The influence of the Sunday School Movement was also considerable. Their founder Thomas Charles recognized the importance of singing. In 1808 there began the great gatherings of Sunday Schools, with large numbers of children and adults joining in processions with singing as they moved to the place of meeting. The hymns that were sung were those used in the regular worship of the chapels. No one had as yet written hymns in Welsh specially for children.

Because of these developments, those who were publishing books on music and editing collections of hymn tunes were doing so in a setting where there were literally thousands of people up and down the land eager to receive their work, to learn the new tunes and to sing them in gatherings great and small. Thus in 1837 Hugh Evans (1790-1853), an animal doctor by profession, brought out the first of nine quarterly parts of *Egwyddorion Peroriaeth* (*The Principles of Music*) especially for the Choral Society of Cerryg-y-Drudion in Denbighshire.

A greater figure altogether was The Reverend Evan Evans (Ieuan Glan Geironydd 1795-1855), one of the best poets of the first half of the 19th century (see page 116). Like the Revd J.D.Edwards he worked and wrote to encourage the congregational singing of the established church. In 1838 he brought out *Y Seraph* (*The Seraph — a collection of sacred tunes in various meters*). The collection is on the whole disappointing in the quality of the tunes and of their harmony. He composed tunes himself and a number of these were published with harmonies by some of the better musicians of the time in a memorial volume that was brought out soon after his death. The best known is GLAN GEIRIONYDD, a tune that survives in both Welsh and English books.

GLAN GEIRIONYDD

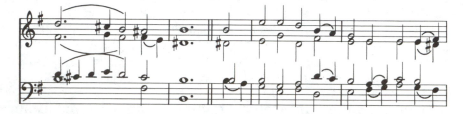

Most of the tunes in *Peroriaeth Hyfryd* (*Sweet Music* 1837) were from English sources, but in preparing the book The Revd John Parry of Chester had received a number of older Welsh tunes from John Roberts, Henllan, who provided the harmonies. Thus this book is the source for a number of important early tunes. LLANF-AIR is by Robert Williams (c1781-1821). He was blind from birth and never moved from Mynydd Ithel, Llanfechell, Anglesey, but he learnt basket making and had a fine voice. A manuscript copy of the tune under the name BETHEL was in existence in his family in 1920.

LLANFAIR

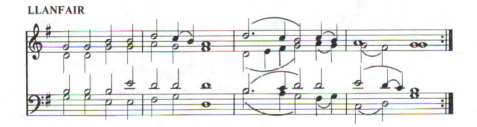

Two tunes written in the same year, 1824, but not published until 1837 were CAERSALEM (Jerusalem) and HYDER (Boldness). Robert Edwards was a native of Mostyn, Flint and he began life as a miller. After moving to Liverpool he worked hard to gain promotion in the Bridgewater Trust that was responsible for the canal of that name. He was in charge of the music of Bedford Street Chapel, (now Princes Road), Liverpool. It is said that he wrote many tunes that were never sung and that CAERSALEM only came to light while he was away ill, when it was found among his papers and learned by the choir. It is now in many English language books all over the world.

CAERSALEM

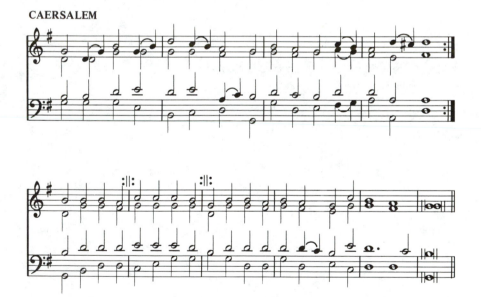

In the same metre is HYDER. The composer was Richard Ellis (1775-1855) a shoemaker from Dolgellau.

HYDER

On the whole the musicians who were bringing out collections were including either tunes from England or tunes of recent Welsh composition. It is in this context that the importance can be seen of *Caniadau y Cyssegr* (*Hymns of the Sanctuary* 1839) in which John Roberts of Henllan (1807-76) brought together 'A Collection of Tunes Old and New, mostly of Welsh composition. Harmonized for four voices!'. His work was important in preserving a number of the tunes whose composers are unknown (see page 154), but his book also preserved some by known composers. David John James (1743-1831) is known by two tunes DORCAS (in the BRAINT 2.88888 meter) and PRISCILLA from this book. John Roberts' own tunes were collected and published by two of his sons at the very end of his life, but they are much less important than his earlier work in preserving the tunes of others.

PRISCILLA

A much greater influence on the singing of the churches in Wales was exercised by the Mills family of Llanidloes in central Wales. The founder of the line was Henry Mills (1757-1820). His musical gifts were recognized by Thomas Charles of Bala who encouraged the local church leadership to place him in charge of the congregational singing of the area, a quite new idea. His son James (1790-1844) continued his work, in particular in the leadership he gave to the Singing Society of Llanidloes, founded in 1834 to teach music to the youth of Bethel Chapel and to improve the music of the worship. James' chief gift was in conducting and teaching though he did compose a number of tunes and anthems. His sturdy tune HOSANNA is still in use in Wales; its metre and accentuation make it difficult to use in any other language.

HOSANNA

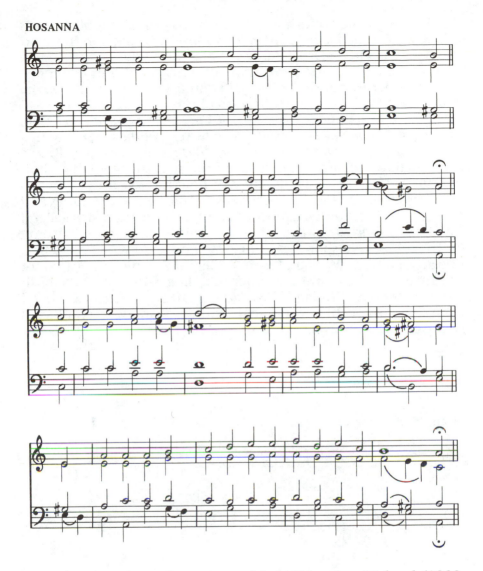

Of much wider influence was his half-brother Richard (1809-44). After leaving school at the age of eleven he learnt the trade of weaver. He started composing at an early age and had a tune published at the age of fifteen. He was twenty-six when he delivered his famous lecture on 'Music' to the Llanidloes Welsh Society, and thereafter he was in much demand as lecturer on that subject. In 1838 Richard's nephew The Revd John Mills (1812-73), well known for his lecturing and writings on music, published his *Gramadeg Cerddoriaeth* (*Grammar of Music*), which for the next twenty years circulated widely in Wales, and had a considerable influence on the new generation of musicians. But the most important contribution of the Mills family to the music of the churches in Wales was the collection of tunes brought out in 1840 by Richard Mills under the title of *Caniadau Seion* (*Songs of Sion, that is a Collection of Tunes suitable to be sung in the worship of God ... arranged in a proper manner for Welsh church music*). In the introduction Richard Mills writes of the necessity he felt to borrow tunes from other lands, though he criticized these tunes as being often unsuitable and ineffective. Among the 214 tunes and 13 anthems there are a number of arrangements from Handel and Haydn together with many English tunes. There are over twenty of the older Welsh tunes, one the best known of which is MEIRIONYDD by William Lloyd (1786-1852) which appeared for the first time here and has reached a large number of English language books. William Lloyd was a farmer and cattle drover from Caernarvonshire who had a good voice and who conducted singing classes in his native district of Llaniestyn.

MEIRIONNYDD

There are a number of tunes by a new generation of Welsh musicians, such as R.H.Prichard, Rosser Beynon and Morris Davies. There is also a tune by J. Ambrose Lloyd, who was to prove one of those who brought a new birth to Welsh congregational music in the second half of the century. Richard Mills himself contributed twenty-nine tunes and seven anthems. Surprisingly there are also a number of the rather weak and superficial tunes that were in the eyes of many pulling down the standard of congregational singing, tunes such as DEVIZES, LINGHAM, CALCUTTA, and LYDIA. A Supplement to *Caniadau Seion* appeared in 1842 with a further 80 tunes and more anthems. There are now hymns for the Sunday School and for the Temperance movement and Friendly Societies. There is an arrangement of the 'Dead March in Saul' (Handel) and a Temperance song to an arrangement of the Minuet from the overture to 'Samson'. There is a second tune by Ambrose Lloyd. In 1842 and 1843 Richard Mills brought out *Yr Arweinydd Cerddorol (The Musical Guide)* in which there are the elements of music, vocal exercises and some guides to composition: in Part II in 1843 there are hymn tunes, anthems and pieces of both a devotional and entertaining nature. In this collection there is a tune of German origin, almost certainly the first to appear in a Welsh hymn collection. The tune is called ALMAEN (Germany), but is best known now in Wales as MANNHEIM, and elsewhere as PASSION CHORALE; Mills ascribes the tune to J.S.Bach. Part III was brought out after Richard's death but was substantially prepared by him. Again there are hymn tunes and anthems, including some Handel choruses. *The Musical Guide* sold nine thousand parts very quickly and did great good in its time. Richard Mills' anthems were frequently sung in the years after his death, but have long since fallen out of use, as, strangely, have his hymn tunes. Undoubtedly *Caniadau Seion* was a landmark on the road to the improvement of congregational singing in Wales. It placed in musicians' hands a wide selection of music from which they could choose the good or the bad. Reading through the collection today gives an interesting insight into what a practical musician in the 1840s thought was necessary and good for the churches. Without his work the improvements that were soon to follow would have been much more difficult.

The Mills family continued active in music after the death of Richard. In 1846 The Revd John Mills and Richard Mills (son of Richard) brought out *Cerddor Eglwysig* (*The Church Musician*) with 101 tunes, including some dozen of the old Welsh tunes, and in 1847 they produced a supplement to it with a further 55 tunes.

Typical of the more general work that was being done is that of Rowland Huw Pritchard (1811-87). He was born near Bala and moved to Holywell in Flintshire to work as an official of the 'Welsh Flannel manufacturing Company'. It is said that he wrote his only famous tune HYFRYDOL (Pleasant, Melodious) at the age of twenty. He published it with others in *Cyfaill y Cantorion* (*The Singers' Friend* 1844), a collection intended for the use of the Sunday School, to wean them from 'empty and defiling songs' to those that are devotional and moral. The tune is so well known that it is worth giving it in its original form for three voices (there were still some musicians at that time who thought that there was something improper in four part harmony). HYFRYDOL shows some sophistication in construction: it is all contained within the range of a sixth; it repeats the first two lines and then moves to a contrasting two lines as if it is going to be a typical AABA pattern; the last two lines are quite new however, with a strong sequential pattern in line seven and only slight hints of derivation from what went before.

HYFRYDOL

At the same time that Richard Mills was working in mid-Wales an even more influential figure was at work in Mold and in Liverpool. John Lloyd (1815-74), usually known by the name he took from 1839 onwards, as John Ambrose Lloyd, was born in Mold and early received lessons in music. He read assiduously in English as well as in Welsh and gave himself a good grounding in the musical classics that were within reach. He composed his first tune WYDDGRUG when he was sixteen, and it has remained in use ever since.

WYDDGRUG

In 1830 John's brother Isaac moved to Liverpool as a school-master and took John with him. In 1835 he joined the Brunswick Road Tabernacle Congregational Chapel and there came under the great preacher Williams of Wern, who brought new life to the congregation and encouragement to John Ambrose Lloyd. In 1841 he moved to the newly founded Chapel, Salem, Brownlow Hill, where he was put in charge of the music. He founded a choir and taught the members to read music, using an early form of Solfa. It became the custom to sing unaccompanied anthems in the service under his direction.

Ambrose Lloyd grew dissatisfied with the tunes sung in the Liverpool chapels. In Tabernacle he prepared a manuscript collection and circulated the tunes among the singers. From 1841 he started in earnest to collect and compose tunes and he brought out *Casgliad o Donau* (*A Collection of Tunes*) in 1843. There are 229 tunes in the collection in 73 metres, together with 8 anthems. There are 28 tunes by Ambrose Lloyd; the older Welsh tunes are poorly represented; there are many English tunes together with tunes by comtemporary Welsh composers. Ambrose Lloyd, like Richard Mills, adapted tunes from the masters, such as those based on 'Lift up your heads' and 'How beautiful are the feet' by Handel, and on 'The Heavens are telling' by Haydn. In 1851 he moved back to North Wales to live, where he made his home in various places till the end of his life. Of his 28 tunes in *Casgliad o Donau* only two (WYDDGRUG and EIFIONYDD) survive in his *Aberth Moliant* (*Sacrifice of Praise*) of 1870. This is itself a sign of his own personal development and of the development of standards in Wales that he himself had done much to promote. In all he wrote some 90 tunes, his mature work being in a majestic and devotional style entirely fitting for use in worship. He wrote 3 Cantatas and 28 anthems, one of which *Teyrnasoedd y ddaear* (The kingdoms of the earth) is to the Welsh the great classic anthem, though to English ears it is very much a pastiche of the 18th century style. One of his finest tunes is GROESWEN, sometimes sung in England to versions of *Meine Hoffnung* such as 'All my hope on God is founded' (Robert Bridges).

GROESWEN

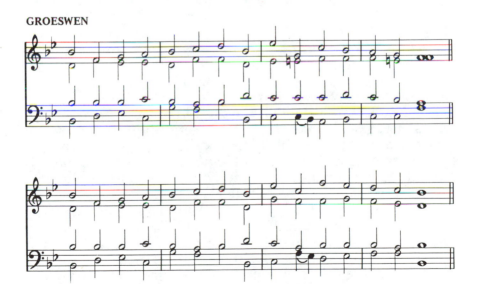

Of the three musicians whose work is generally recognized as having given a new birth to the hymn singing of Wales, Ambrose Lloyd was the first to gain recognition. Their influence did not spread immediately, and work similar to that of the early part of the century continued to be produced, some of it contributing actively in preparing the ground for the more important figures.

William Jacob (1777-1845) was the leader of the singing in Trefynnon (Holywell) in North Wales for many years, and towards the very end of his life brought out *Eos Cymru* (*The Nightingale of Wales* 1844), a collection of material typical of the period, with tunes, chants and anthems ('Worthy is the Lamb' appeared here in Welsh for the first time). The tune HUDDERSFIELD appeared in a Welsh collection here for the first time; it became very popular with congregations despite opposition by the best musicians.

Thomas Williams (1807-94), better known as 'Hafrenydd' was as important for his contribution to the choral singing of Wales as he was to its hymns. In 1846 he brought out the first of eight parts of *Y Salmydd·Cenedlaethol* (*The National Psalmist*), a collection of music for the established church, with tunes, anthems and items of sacred music from Handel, Haydn, Mozart, Beethoven, Pleyel and others. He also translated for this series *Wilhelm's Method of Singing,* which became the basis of John Hullah's method of teaching singing and thus an influence on the development of Solfa. His choice of hymn tunes was good; Ambrose Lloyd wrote 4 tunes specially for him: he enlisted the help of notable English church musicians, among them W.H. Havergal, and H.J. Gauntlett, who assisted in the editing. Even more influential was *Ceinion Cerddoriaeth* (*Jewels of Music*) which he brought out in 1852. The first part contained 220 tunes in 68 meters; the second volume contained 70 anthems and choruses, some by Welsh composers, but most of them by the great masters, including choruses from 'Messiah', 'Samson', 'Israel in Egypt' and the

'Dettingen Te Deum' by Handel, and from Haydn's 'Creation'. It took time for Welsh choirs to develop the skills necessary to sing these choruses, so that the influence of this collection was not immediate, but by the end of his long life he was able to see the fruit of the seed that had been sown in 1852.

Rosser Beynon (1811-76) worked hard in the cause of church music in the South. He had little early education and went to work in the iron foundry at the age of 8. But by means of attendance at evening schools and private study he became a most proficient musician and an acknowledged leader in South Wales. In 1845 he began to bring out in parts *Telyn Seion* (*Zion's Harp*); he published the whole in one volume in 1848. It includes 130 tunes in over 100 metres, 22 anthems and choruses and short pieces for Sunday Schools. His taste was good and he would have nothing to do with the poor quality tunes that were so popular at the time. He included many of the better tunes that were by then being written including a number by Ambrose Lloyd, who wrote GROESWEN especially for this collection. Rosser Beynon included metronome markings for the first time in Wales, with an account at the end of the book of the working of the Maelzel metronome.

Joseph David Jones (1827-70) made his most important contribution to Welsh congregational singing by his association in later life with Tanymarian (see page 191). He was largely self-taught in music. He had great natural gifts as a teacher; he studied teaching for 6 months in London where he qualified in 1851 and thus was able to take up the profession for the rest of his life. He published *Y Perganiedydd* (*The Sweet Songster*) in 1846 when he was only 19, and in it appeared CAPEL Y DDOL his best known tune. He made a profit on the book and this financed some of his education. The style of hymn tune that he favoured was simple and fluent, a great contrast to the florid tunes popularly sung. He brought out a number of other collections; he won prizes in Eisteddfod competitions for his compositions, and was one of the first true songwriters in Wales.

CAPEL Y DDOL

Griffiths Harris (1813-92) was a shopkeeper by trade, and a good musician, being the leader of the singing in the Methodist Chapel in Carmarthen and conductor of the town choir. In 1849 he brought out *Halelwiah* and in 1855 *Halelwiah Drachefn* (*Haleeluia Again*). The second volume is important because of his emphasis on the old Welsh tunes, in particular those named in the 1811 edition of the hymns of William Williams Pantycelyn. That is not to say that there are not a great number of poor tunes too in these collections.

In 1852 The Revd Robert Williams brought out *Cydymaith yr Addolydd* (*The Worshipper's Vade Meum*) for the use of the Wesleyan Methodists in Wales. The music was edited by Thomas Jones (1823-1904, known as ' Canrhawdfardd'), a prolific writer and composer. In the same year William Owen of Prysgol (1813-93) brought out *Y Perl Cerddorol* (*The Musical Pearl*). He grew up near Bethesda in North Wales and went to work in the slate quarry at the age of ten. He lived near the church of St Anne and used to take every opportunity to hear the organist playing. He became a good musician and began to compose when quite young. He contributed many tunes to the Temperance movement. He gained the name 'Prysgol', by which he is most widely known, when he moved to the village of that name not far from Caernarvon. Some of his tunes were very popular, but they were in a style that fell out of favour under the reforms in music that gradually found favour in Wales. One tune remains popular and has travelled world-wide, BRYN CALFARIA. It was recognized by Vaughan Williams who included it in *English Hymnal* and wrote a powerful Prelude for Organ on it. He did however civilize line five somewhat, making it less earthy in its expression, but not depriving it of its essential power. Most English language books accept this version; some of these also move the bar-lines and this does change the nature of the tune by diminishing the driving power of the rhythm. This is the version of the tune that is best known in Wales.

BRYN CALFARIA

*Note: this version still appears in contemporary Welsh books. Others follow English editors from *English Hymnal* 1906 onwards in having all voices sing continuously throughout.

John Roberts (1806-79) is likewise known for one tune. He wrote ALEXANDER when he was only eighteen and it had appeared several times without any composer's name before it appeared in John Roberts' own collection *Perorydd y Cysegr* (*The Musician of the Sanctuary* 1853). He was born near Bala and moved to Aberystwyth to take up his trade as a carver. He studied music in his spare time and became well known in the district. He moved in 1855 to Aberdar and that is the name by which he is distinguished from the many other John Roberts who were church musicians. The tune is usually sung in a later more sophisticated harmonization; it is given here as it appears in *Caniadau Seion*.

ALEXANDER

Y Blwch Cerddorol (The Musical Casket 1854) differed from other books in that its 84 tunes were entirely by Welsh composers. The editor Thomas Davies (1810?-73?) was a farmer in Glamorgan who travelled that area teaching singing. His own tunes appear in other collections. The tune that survives in use from the 100 in this book is DYFFRYN BACA (The Valley of Baca) by David Richards (1835-1906) who emigrated to Wilksbarre, Pennsylvania.

DYFFRYN BACA

Morris Davies (1796-1876) was member of an older generation who lived to see great changes in congregational music in Wales and to contribute to them by his tunes, his editing and his writings on music. For most of his working life he was a schoolmaster. He began collecting hymn tunes in 1815 and it was from this source that Richard Mills and Griffith Harris took some of the old Welsh tunes that appear in their collections. In 1860 Morris Davies published *Jeduthun*, with 106 tunes, 10 of them of his own composition. Of his tunes only RHOSLAN survives in use.

RHOS - LAN

The life story of David Richards (1822-1900) is typical of many enterprising young men at that time. He was born on a farm in Pembrokeshire and moved as a young man to work in a colliery in Blaenau, Monmouthshire. There he led the music in the Congregational chapel, Berea, where he taught music on the principles of

Hullah. He went to college in 1851 and was ordained in 1855 to be minister of Siloam, Llanelli. It was there that he collected the hymn tunes that the older members of the congregation sang. After his move to Caerphilly in 1862 he published these in *Swn Addoli* (*The Sound of Worship* 1862). It is a valuable resource book to anyone studying the history of Welsh hymn tunes.

These then were the pioneers in music who were the first to lead Wales into a wider appreciation of singing and music in general and to bring into use a wider repertoire of tunes. It must be remembered that they continued to do this against considerable opposition. The battle was fought out in the local churches, in their Society meetings and in Sunday School discussions. But a good reflection of these controversies can be seen in the introductions that were written to the collections of tunes and above all in articles that appeared in the periodicals of the time. The early years of the 19th century saw a number of periodicals launched. Some of them had a very short life: some of them appeared intermittently as their publisher faced financial problems and overcame them; some few lasted for many decades. Some of them were national and political in their general interest; many were religious and often sprang from an affiliation to a particular denomination. It was in these periodicals that tunes were often given their first publication, but even more important it was here in articles and in correspondence that the whole matter of what was proper to sing in worship was thrashed out over and over again throughout the early decades of the century. The concerns remain the same. There is the evergreen matter of the new over against the old, the well-tried against the new, whether it be in the matter of tunes or even new meters. But there are Welsh concerns that may not be so familiar. In some circles it was a particular concern that especially in the Singing Societies it was possible for those who had not professed the faith to join in the praise of God. This was quite abhorrent to some and quite natural to others since it could lead to faith in those who sang. Some were worried that there were Christians who were concerning themselves about the correctness of the music and its quality when it was not at all clear that there was any direction in Scripture on these matters. 'Sing with the Spirit and with the understanding' was a favourite quotation which had to be widely extended to cover the emphasis that the musicians gave to the observance of the proper rules and received taste. Is there anything in our faith that compels us to sing in an orderly manner? The answer given to this is usually that God is a God of order not of disorder. There were frequent complaints of congregations singing different versions of the tune simultaneously; of them singing out of time and tune with each other; of them beginning the next verse in one part of the congregation before others have finished the last: it was generally decided that all these things are disorderly and not suited to the worship of a God of order. We need to work for dignity and order in our worship. A further question was, if knowledge of music is godly and desirable, how should it be spread? The way generally favoured was the natural one of appointing the most able musician to make a study of the art and to teach others. This is what clearly was happening in the Singing Societies: Day School teachers were particularly encouraged to undertake this. Should singing from notes be allowed? This was much disputed, but since the reading of words was allowed, why not the reading of music? and if good order was required, then here was a well tried way to obtain it. Whether the singing should be of the melody only, in harmony in three parts, or in harmony in four parts was long debated. For a long time even when singing of parts was allowed the hymns were sung in only three parts. Gradually, as a knowledge of the musical world outside Wales became more widespread, the general convention gained ground that singing should be in four parts. The Bible could not be called into that argument with any conviction, any more than it could over that question of where the singers should stand in the church. Over the matter of instruments in church the Bible could be quoted, with some writers instancing the many references in the Old Testament to a wide variety of instruments, while others asserted that under the New Covenant matters were quite different and that things of the fleshly 'body of death' should be put away and that only the human voice was proper in worship.

As late as 1844 The Revd D. Lloyd Isaac, a Baptist Minister thought of as something of an authority on such matters, was being appealed to in *Seren Gomer* (*Gomer's Star,* a very long running periodical) to pronounce on all these matters. In a long letter he reproves both the young people in the congregation that wish to have it all their own way with new hymns and the old members who will have none of them. The young must not reduce the older members to silence by including nothing but the new tunes: the old must not be stubborn, but must recognize the 'march of

188

intellect' (he uses the English phrase). There should be compromise, the old and the new used side by side. Satan is at work and has stolen many good tunes and all the instruments of music. They are not the hairsbreadth worse (to translate his words) because of this. Away with prejudice and blindness and that 'ultra' sanctity which is without order, without taste and is stubborn! Bring back to the sanctuary every instrument and tune that is suitable to a truly 'sacred music'. The singing should be warm and full of spirit. God can tolerate mistakes, a cracked voice, singing out of time. What is loathsome to God is lukewarmness, pride and hypocrisy. It is quite improper to sit dozing while the song of praise is rising about the altar. In the words of Nehemiah 'Rise up and praise the Lord'.

Even such vigorous writing could not sweep away all objections overnight. The Welsh have found it necessary to invent a phrase to describe the arguments and controversies that continually arise over music, particularly church music, *cythraul y canu*. It is difficult to translate. *Cythraul* is 'the devil' and *y canu* here means 'of the singing', and the phrase is about the devil that seems to get into church musicians when they begin to disagree about the music, and about who is to do what in church. It is not new, or confined to the Welsh, but it is helpful to realize, in looking at the steady progress of congregational singing in Wales, that it took place against a background of argument, at times heated argument.

The Rebirth of Welsh Hymn singing

The story so far has been one of steady progress, won painfully by the hard work of many men, some of them very gifted, but none of them with either the ability or the opportunity to make the revolution come about that was necessary. Many things conspired together in the end to make that possible, but three men were the catalysts of change. John Ambrose Lloyd (1815-74) has already been mentioned. Being the oldest of the three his work overlapped that of the earlier generation. The others were Edward Stephen (1822-85), always known as 'Tanymarian', and John Roberts (1822-77) always known as 'Ieuan Gwyllt'.

Tanymarian

Tanymarian's name was Edward Jones but on going to college he found another Edward Jones among the students and he took his grandfather's name 'Stephen' to distinguish himself and the 'Jones' came to be dropped. His father was a singer and harp player and his mother was also a good singer. He went with his brother William into the business of clothier and while learning the craft from Joseph Jones, learnt a great deal about music from him too. At the age of 18 he began preaching in Saron Congregational Chapel, Ffestiniog. In 1843 he went to the Congregational College at Bala, and while at college set about learning music as well as theology. In 1847 he was appointed as minister of Horeb Chapel, Dywgyfylchi, on the North Wales coast between Penmaenmawr and Conway. In his ten years there he became well known all over Wales as a preacher, poet, lecturer, writer and musician. Between January 1851 and May 1852 he wrote *Ystorm Tiberias* (The Storm on the Sea of Tiberias), an oratorio, the first work of its kind to be written by a Welshman. He brought it out in 1855 in seven instalments. The work received some performances up and down the country, and for many years the choruses were frequently set pieces for choral competitions in Welsh *eisteddfodau*. In a careful essay on the work, written shortly after his death for the memorial volume published in 1886, D. Emlyn Evans, one of the leading musicians of the next generation, notes the composer's debt to Handel, natural in the composer of an oratorio, and judges in general that Tanymarian was a good composer of choruses, but that the solos and duets did not reach the same standard. At the very end of his life Tanymarian revised the work, and according to Emlyn Evans, made great improvements in the solo work. The revised version was published in 1887. In its original form the accompaniment was for keyboard, but Emlyn Evans himself produced an orchestration. There is clearly a certain amount of special pleading in this essay: a first work of this kind by a composer entirely out of reach of the advantages of training that any composer needs, and unable even to reach performances of the great works, must be to a certain extent primitive. That does not diminish the size of the achievement in writing it at all, and the breadth of vision of a man who could set about such a task in the circumstances of the time. He did not in fact ever return to the form. He composed anthems, glees, part songs and solo songs, but he clearly did not give time to developing his composition after his first huge effort.

In 1856 he accepted the invitation to move to be minister of the churches of Bethlehem and Carmel, Llanllechid, not far from Bangor. It was then that he moved into the house called 'Tanymarian' by which name he came to be known thereafter. In 1859 he began the work through which, whatever needs to be said about his oratorio, he made his greatest mark on Welsh music. In that year he took over the editorship of *Cerddor y Cysegr (Musician of the Sanctuary)*, a collection of hymns and tunes, after three parts had appeared under the editorship of Robert Williams of Pentre Berw, Anglesey. The book was notable in that for the first time in Welsh the words and the tunes appeared in the same volume. The circumstances show clearly that the collection was not planned by Tanymarian, although some of the marks of his editorship are visible. There are tunes harmonized by him, in a clean, fresh style, with the emphasis on singable parts in all voices. He was known to castigate editors who included too many of their own tunes: there is not one of his tunes in this collection. This was also due to the respect he had for the form, which in his judgement is a particularly difficult one since it calls for 'an ability, skill, and a special genius to compose a tune worthy of the sanctuary'. For his contributions to this form one turns to *Llyfr Tonau ac Emynau (The Book of Tunes and Hymns* 1869) and its Second Volume of 1879. Here again, as the title shows, are words and music, this time with several hymns set to be sung to most tunes. This makes necessary that distinctive feature of almost every Welsh hymn book since then, that the words and the tunes are numbered separately. There are 555 Welsh hymns and 19 English in the 1869 volume, with 196 tunes, and a further 342 hymns in the second volume, with 107 tunes. *Cerddor y Cysegr* was a small, cheaply produced book. This is a handsome volume, easily readable with a well laid-out, almost square page, very like its contemporary in England *Hymns Ancient and Modern*. The work on the first volume was shared with J. D. Jones (see page 181) who is said to have done most of the work in choosing and arranging the tunes. It is appropriate therefore that one of the finest of the Welsh tunes, his GWALCHMAI should have appeared here. It is the ideal antidote to the notion that a truly Welsh tune is in the minor and mournful; this tune sings like the dawn chorus. Tanymarian's ideal of singable lines in all parts is realized here, particularly in its original version, usually 'corrected' in the English books in which it widely appears, to remove a small technical fault in the part writing.

GWALCHMAI

Tanymarian was solely responsible for the second volume in 1879, J.D. Jones having died in 1870. There were only two of his tunes in the first volume: this time there were more, but even here only nine, his greatest contribution being the fine arrangements of the older Welsh tunes, such as CAERLLYGOED, DINIWEIDRWYDD, MORIAH and HYDER. His most popular tune is certainly TANYMARIAN. It is surprising, since it is in a meter fairly common in English, that it has not traveled outside Wales. It certainly does have a sombre colour, but some texts need that. Melodically there is sufficient repetition to be memorable, but with a constant development which prevents boredom, and there is a fine flight of melody in the last two lines.

TANYMARIAN

Emlyn Evans, writing in the memorial volume to Tanymarian, claims that his most distnctive voice is to be heard in GLAN DWYRYD. It is certainly a striking piece, but so much developed that it is more like a tiny anthem — indeed it is much more interesting than the anthems by Tanymarian published in the memorial volume.

GLAN DWYRYD

Tanymarian was not a purist. The next generation criticized him for the inclusion of such tunes as THE LAST ROSE OF SUMMER, ROUSSEAU'S DREAM, and DEAD MARCH IN SAUL. He even included (albeit in an appendix) HUDDERSFIELD (a tune which Emlyn Evans would refuse to conduct when asked to do so as part of a hymn singing festival). But his critics were able to take this stance only because Tanymarian's generation had won that high critical ground for them, and in any case these tunes were in the minority in his book and totally overshadowed by the truly great tunes in fine arrangements that predominated. *Llyfr Tonau ac Emynau* served the congregational chapels until almost the end of the century. Tanymarian himself served the cause of Welsh hymn singing by his writing and conducting as well as by his editing. He played his part in the growth of the *Cymanfa Ganu* (Singing Meeting). He personally favoured the growth of choirs in the Welsh chapels, much opposed though this was by other leaders of the reform movement in singing, who wanted all the music to be congregational. Tanymarian left his mark in all those chapels built after 1860 which have seats for the choir. It became the custom either to build them above and behind the pulpit, or, more commonly, to one side in the front, near the *Sêt Fawr* (Big Seat) where they were known as the *Sêt Ganu* (Singing Seat). Even more he left his mark on the collective musical mind of the Welsh. He was one of those who defined for them the nature of the Welsh Hymn tune.

Ieuan Gwyllt

But the greatest influence of all in the decades in the middle of the century when so much was happening to the music of Wales was John Roberts (1822-77) aways known by the pen name that he gave himself in a poetry competition in his youth, 'Ieuan Gwyllt' ('Ieuan' is 'John', and 'Gwyllt' is 'Wild', but the words do not quite mean 'Wild John' in the grammatical forms used, more 'John Wild'). Wild he was not. A man of restless energy he certainly was.

He was born in mid-Wales, not far from Aberystwyth; his mother was a good singer and his father was the leader of the singing in the chapel. In 1823 the family moved to Aberystwyth, and again in 1829 to Pistyllgwyn in the Melindwr valley, not far from Aberystwyth. In 1842 John obtained a place as a clerk in pharmacy in Aberystwyth. In 1844 he was appointed schoolmaster in a local school, but after a few months he went to the Borough Road Normal School in London to be trained as a teacher. He failed to get a certificate, probably because of ill health, but on returning in 1845 he opened the 'British School' in Aberystwyth. After only nine months he gave up the school and went to work for a solicitor, and there he stayed for seven years. In 1852 he made the most momentous move in his life. He went to Liverpool as assistant editor of *Yr Amserau* (*The Times*), finding himself almost immediately in sole charge. He appears to have been a natural journalist, but he was already aware of a calling to preach and he gave his first sermon in 1856 in Runcorn. He stayed with *Yr Amserau* until 1858 when he moved to Aberdar in South Wales as Editor of *Y Gwladgarwr* (*The Patriot*). In 1859 he married and he accepted the invitation to be the minister of a Calvinistic Methodist Church in Merthyr Tydfil. In 1865 he accepted the call to be minister of Capel Coch, Llanberis, where he remained until his retirement in 1869, when he went to live at Llangfaglan near Caernarvon, where he died in 1877. This would be a full enough career for most men, but it is only the framework on which the main fabric of Ieuan Gwyllt's life was worked. He was an influential journalist, with a reputation for writing strongly worded editorials in the liberal interest, castigating those responsible for the manifest evils of a time when there was great industrial growth with little responsibility being shown by those who made the profits for the welfare of the workers and their families. But his main work was with the music of the church: he collected and edited hymn tunes; he produced periodicals for musicians; he lectured and preached to raise the people's consciousness of the need for better standards in worship; he judged *eisteddfodau* and conducted musical festivals; indeed he created the 'Cymanfa Ganu' as it is now known.

He wrote verses in his early years, and some, clearly for use in the Sunday School, have survived. He began to compose early too and a tune HAFILA, written before he was fifteen, was published in a periodical in 1839. It is interesting to see that it was written in the older manner for three voices. It was in his years as a solicitor's clerk in Aberystwyh that he got his most important musical training and had some contact with the Mills family of Llanidloes. He took part in every section of chapel life and found himself at times in conflict with the leaders of the community who saw in this rough young man from the country something of an upstart to be kept in place. This is probably why, when he was examined as a possible candidate for the ministry, he was refused. In 1852, while still in Aberystwyth, he formed a partnership with three friends to bring out a monthly periodical called *Blodau Cerdd* (*Flowers of Music*), with himself as editor. The first four issues were printed in Aberystwyth, the last three in Llanidloes. The aim of the publication was to give simple instruction in music with the aim of improving church music. Much of the instruction was given in the form of a catechism or dialogue. There were original hymns and translations together with tunes, including some by Ambrose Lloyd. The aims of the venture were high. Looking back however at *Blodau Cerdd* from the vantage of his later achievements it is possible to wonder that Ieuan Gwyllt's standards were in fact so low at that period. The key to this was the narrow experience he had so far had. This was to be remedied immediately.

As Ambrose Lloyd had found twenty years earlier, Liverpool was part of a much wider world in every kind of way, not least in the realm of music. Ieuan Gwyllt became a member of Rose Place Church and was in charge of the singing for a period, and worked alongside Eleazar Roberts (1825-1912), whose work with Tonic Sol-fa was shortly afterwards to be so important in Wales. He was for a time a member of the Liverpool Philharmonic Society; he would travel far to attend concerts and recitals, sometimes to London, and after these he would write a column about them in *Yr Amserau*. He began to be known as a judge at competitions and as a conductor at such events as the Temperance Musical Festivals. His occasional preaching also took him up and down the country. He had for years been keeping a notebook of tunes, and now he began to make it known that he intended to publish a collection of them. He sought his material in many directions, but was especially concerned to look at the sacred music of Germany. This interest is reflected in an article that he wrote in 1857 for the *Traethodydd* (*The Essayist*) on 'Mendelssohn, his life and work' as the first of a series on the great German composers.

He was not happy however in Liverpool. He was lonely. His radical politics separated him from many chapel people and his very involvement in journalism from others. His reforming zeal in music was not always well received, a hard lesson that he was to be learning for the rest of his life. Everything was not well in the office of the newspaper and it was with relief that he moved to Aberdar to take over the editorship of *Y Gwladgarwr*. Four important things happened within the space of a year. As soon as he was settled in Aberdar he married Miss Jane Richards of Aberystwyth. Three months later in April 1859 there appeared his *Llyfr Tonau Cynulleidfaol* (*The Book of Congregational Tunes*). Two years earlier he had been writing to 'My Anwyl Jane' (My Dear Jane) that the book was nearing completion, saying that it would cost him £300 to bring out 3,000 copies, but that after that it would cost only £30 a thousand. In three years it sold 17,000 copies. That was the measure of the great expectation that there was surrounding it and the enthusiasm with which it was received.

The book contained 220 tunes printed in four vocal parts in open score with the tune in the top part. He later produced an appendix of a further 20 tunes or variant versions of tunes already in the book. The difference between the tunes chosen for this book and the tunes of 1852 is huge. He is, as his preface shows, trying to show to the people of Wales how unsuitable are so many of the tunes in circulation for the worship of God; he is giving them the opportunity to replace them with tunes that are at the same time simple, majestic and devotional; he is proposing a campaign of education, with regular singing meetings in every church, organized by the church, at which every member is expected to be present to learn the tunes for the services and to practise them well. He believed that music should be one of the subjects of study for every minister, so that they can read the tunes and have the background both to exhort the church in sermons on the singing of God's praises and to lead discussions on the subject. At the beginning of January 1859 the first *Cymanfa Ganu* was held, in Aberdar, using the proof sheets of the book which had not yet appeared. As has been seen, the ground had been prepared for the *Cymanfa Ganu* in the Temperance Society meetings since the beginning of that movement in 1835. What congregational singing needed was a prophet, a charismatic figure to carry a strong message. Ieuan Gwyllt was such a man and had provided in his collection of tunes the means by which the movement could go forward. By 1861 Unions of Congregational Singing were springing up all over the country, with many of them inviting Ieuan Gwyllt to lecture to them and to conduct their singing.

There was a fourth important happening in the year 1858-59. Unlike the situation in Liverpool he had found himself immediately officially recognized as a preacher in the Calvinistic Methodist connexion in South Wales. Now he accepted the call to be the minister of Pant-tywyll Chapel, Merthyr. In 1861 he was fully ordained to the work of ministry. It was in many ways a strange move. His editorial writings showed the preacher in him as he campaigned against the evils of contemporary society. In many ways the pulpit provided a smaller audience than the weekly newspaper: he was not nearly as fluent a preacher as he was a writer. But the pulpit drew him and to the ministry he went. That was not to say that his gifts as an editor and writer were to be lost to the Church and to music. Far from it. Already in early 1859 there had started to appear as a monthly publication *Telyn y Plant* (*The Children's Harp*) under the editorship of The Revd Thomas Levi and Ieuan Gwyllt. It continued in existence until 1861 when it was taken into *Trysorfa'r Plant* (*The Children's Treasury*) in which Ieuan Gwyllt continued to contribute a music section. In March 1861 there appeared the first number of *Y Cerddor Cymraeg* (*The Welsh Musician*) for which Ieuan Gwyllt was totally responsible for the first four years of its existence. It was full of musical news, reports and articles, there was an educational series on the elements of music and on Tonic Sol-fa, and each month it contained compositions by Welsh composers, edited by Ieuan Gwyllt. In 1865 the publishers Hughes and Son of Wrexham took over *Y Cerddor Cymraeg* but Ieuan Gwyllt continued as its editor.

Tonic Sol-fa

Tonic Sol-fa has already been mentioned and it is now necessary to trace its contribution to the rebirth of congregational
singing in Wales. The system had its beginning in a meeting of
friends of the Sunday School Movement in Hull in 1841. There
the Revd John Curwen was urged to bring out a simple method of
learning to read music. Curwen was already engaged in teaching
children to sing, and, basing his scheme on the traditional syllables for the degrees of the scale and on the work of Hullah, he
produced the Tonic Sol-fa scheme with the movable 'doh'. In
1843 Curwen published his *Grammar of Vocal Music* and established a movement to promote Tonic Solfa in 1853. The system
was so successful that Curwen gave up the ministry to devote
himself fully to the work. There are stories of a number of individuals in Wales mastering the system in its early days. The first class
to teach Tonic Sol-fa seems to have been held by David Nicholas
of Cwmafon, Port Talbot, in his own house in 1852. The Revd
Cynffig Davies held the first class in Glamorgan in 1854 and did a
great deal for the movement by translating Curwen's teaching
material into Welsh.

In 1860 John Curwen visited Liverpool to lecture and to expound the Tonic Sol-fa system. Eleazar Roberts and his friend
John Edwards were convinced of its worth and they began to
teach it to the children of the Sunday Schools in Liverpool. After
demonstrations in Liverpool they toured many parts of Wales
demonstrating how useful the system was in enabling children to
sight-read music and to take down tunes from dictation. The
sheer effectiveness of the system overcame the reluctance of many
of the older musicians. Curwen gave permission to Eleazar Roberts to write a series of letters to *Y Cerddor Cymraeg* setting out the
system; ten of these appeared in 1861-2. In 1861 there appeared *Y
Llawlyfr i ddysgu y Tonic Sol-ffa* (*The handbook on the teaching of
Tonic Sol-fa*). In the same year there appeared a book of hymns
and tunes for the Sunday School in Solfa, the first musical publication in Welsh in Solfa. Four more parts to this book appeared,
and the whole collection went through many reprints, remaining
in use for half a century. Eleazar Roberts toured Wales teaching
the system and founding music classes. He argued that it was as
proper to have music classes as part of the Sunday School as it was
to have reading classes: when both skills were mastered the ordinary people would be able to read their hymn book, words and

music together. By 1866 there was hardly a Sunday School in the whole of Wales that did not have a Sol-fa class in it. Ieuan Gwyllt seems to have been slow to believe in the value of the system, but once he had been convinced he threw his great energy into promoting it. In 1863 he brought out his *Llyfr Tonau Cynulleidfaol in Sol-fa, and pieces in Sol-fa began to appear in Y Cerddor Cymraeg.* In 1869 he issued the first number of a new periodical, *Cerddor y Tonic Sol-ffa* (*The Tonic Solfa Musician*), and continued as its editor until 1874. Like many other ministers he taught classes in Sol-fa; in Llanberis he had a class of 150. There can be no doubt that the introduction of Sol-fa enormously aided the improvement in the congregational singing that Ieuan Gwyllt and others were working to gain. Such was the attendance at Sunday School that it seemed that a whole nation was learning to read music. Even many of that 50% who did not attend worship regularly in Wales, even at the height of the popularity of the chapels, had been taught Sol-fa at school or at Sunday School. Though there may be reservations about the usefulness of the system in some kinds of music, there can be no doubt of its effectiveness for hymn tunes. The majority of chapel goers in Wales still sing from Sol-fa books; its use makes accessible for worship a far greater repertoire of tunes than is seen under other conditions. Its very weakness, the fact that it makes the singer think from chord to chord rather than in the curve of a musical phrase visible on paper as in the 'Old Notation', has helped to create a certain style of singing in Welsh.

Ieuan Gwyllt - the final years

Thus Ieuan Gwyllt was able to see a further great surge of interest in the work that he had set under way. But his activities were by no means at an end. In 1865 he had moved to Llanberis and then in 1869 to retirement near Caernarvon. In 1871 he undertook the editorship of the denominational paper *Y Goleuad* (*Illumination*). The old fire was there in his writings, but it is possible that this was not entirely to the taste of those in control of the paper and he resigned after barely a year. Thus he was free for the final, rather strange chapter of his life. In 1874 the American evangelists Sankey and Moody came to Britain. Ieuan Gwyllt went to Edinburgh to hear them and later to Liverpool where he met them. He came strongly under their influence. Whereas he had been a slow and careful preacher he began to preach with fire. Even more astonishing, he was swept away by the music of the musician of the pair, Sankey. The songs and hymns which Sankey sang had an appeal to the audience for which they were intended which is fairly easy to understand. They were aimed not at the educated and prosperous, who in the main made up the church congregations of England, but at the great mass of people in the newly industrialized cities, living in desperately poor conditions, uprooted largely from their places of origin and with their own music now to be found in the music hall rather than in the folksong. What however was it in this music, with its rudimentary harmony and stilted melodies, that had such an effect on Ieuan Gwyllt, who had campaigned for most of his life against such trivialities in worship? It is impossible to say for sure. Here however, in the work of Sankey and Moody, was a ministry that gave a full place to a music that people really wanted to sing. Here were songs that the Sunday School would be able to sing and to sing easily. Here were songs that spoke to the kind of people whose causes Ieuan Gwyllt had espoused in the industrial South. It must be remembered too that it was to become a minister in a great Revival tradition that Ieuan Gwyllt had left a successful career as a journalist. Here were songs that sang the gospel, simply and directly. At any rate at the end of 1874 he published his first collection of translations and arrangments of the Sankey and Moody material under the title *Swn y Jiwbili* (*The Sound of Jubilee*). He published six parts and after a fairly slow beginning the various parts had sold nearly half a million copies by 1934. This does not take into account the sales of the collected edition. It is claimed that Ieuan Gwyllt's translations are better in quality, richer in language and finer in poetic skills than the originals. He did not live to see that in *Swn y Jiwbili* he had an even greater publishing success than in his great book of hymn tunes.

It would be difficult therefore to know what best he himself would wish to be remembered by.

The judgement of the larger musical world would be that he was a fine collector and editor of tunes, with a tremendous flair for the promotion of the cause of better church music by the written word and in his conducting. His own compositions do not reach the level that he expected of others. Few of his tunes have the real spark in them; he seems to be overawed by his favourite models, the German chorales in their most foursquare form, and his tunes move in a pedestrian way. He does find something more in RHEIDOL. It is a pity that the metre is one difficult to use in English.

RHEIDOL

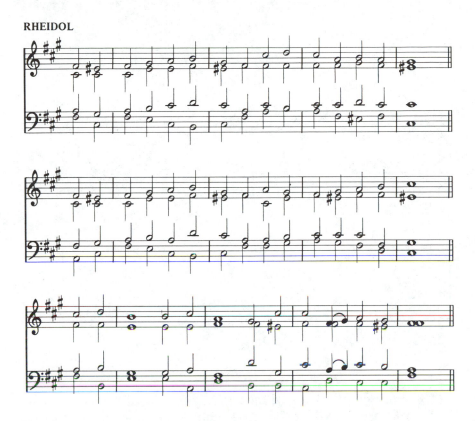

If it has to be said that most of his tunes fall below the standard of the best Welsh tunes it is surprising that one of his tunes has received extravagant praise. Sir Henry Hadow claimed that MOAB was one of the six best hymn tunes in the world. It is true that it has one of the most powerful moments in all hymnody in its daring second line (edited out, quite unbelievably, in the English *Methodist Hymn Book* 1933), and that its architecture is immensely strong, building to a fine climax in line seven. Its meter is not well supplied with words in English, and its inclusion in an English language book is likely to depend on whether the words 'Far off I see the goal' are seen to be needed.

MOAB

The flowering of the Welsh Hymn tune

The effect of the work of Ieuan Gwyllt and to a less extent of John Ambrose Lloyd and Tanymarian was to give to the rich growth of Welsh hymn tune composition a vigorous pruning. The taste of Ieuan Gwyllt was severe and serious at the time that he was collecting his book of tunes. Perhaps one explanation of the strange exploration at the end of his life into the hymns of Sankey is that he felt a need for something in hymnody that was more flexible, that was more of the heart. He had discovered the German Chorale, which was to be his great model, when its form was at its most dull, with its earlier, lively rhythms reduced to a monotonous four beats in the bar. His own tunes reflect that and are less than successul because of it. As a discipline to be imposed on the Welsh hymn however at this point it could not have been bettered. In the same year that his *Llyfr Tonau Cynulledfaol* came out a revival movement was sweeping across the chapels of Wales. This kind of renewed warmth of faith has often led to a lowering of musical standards. With the zeal for the renewal of the music of worship at its height at the same time the effect was the reverse. There was a tremendous flowering of tune composition. There was no great renewal of text writing, as has been seen. Hymns were written that mean a great deal to worshippers in Welsh, but nothing that makes a claim to the attention of those outside Wales. With the tunes it is quite different. Many of the tunes that have become best known outside Wales had already been published before this time. Of the tunes that were written in this period of the great flowering of the Welsh hymn tune there are scores that deserve attention, whether for their potential usefulness outside Wales or for their intrinsic quality as hymntunes.

The first generation after the 'Rebirth'

Three names are associated with the continuation of the work of the generation that brought about the 'Dadeni' — the rebirth of Welsh hymnody.

The bridge from the older generation was David Lewis who was only a little younger than Ieuan Gwyllt (1828-1908) but outlived him considerably. His father was an assiduous collector and arranger of the old Welsh melodies and he followed in the same path. He was in fact taught music by the same Thomas Jenkins who taught Ieuan Gwyllt. He was composing at the age of 15. He won many prizes for hynn tunes. Many of his compositions were published in the musical periodicals of the time. He is credited with the chief responsibility with W.A. Williams (Gwilym Gwent 1838-91) for the editing of the music of *Llwybraur Moliant* (*The Paths of Praise* 1872). This was the book in which LLANGLOFFAN was first published (see page 160).

John Thomas, Llanwrtyd

John Thomas (1839-1921) was usually known until 1871 as 'John Thomas, Blaenannerch', from the place of his birth. On his marriage he moved to Llanwrtyd, by which name he was known for the rest of his life. He was apprenticed to a shop in Castellnewydd Emlyn (Newcastle Emlyn), but returned to his father's shop because of ill health. In 1871 he took over the Post Office in Llanwrtyd. He preserved an unusually close friendship with David Lewis, although over ten years his junior, comparing notes with him, in letters that still survive, on the results of competitions and the like. He won prizes for his compositions in *eisteddfodau* in his earlier years, but after he was thirty he concentrated on poetry. He became one of the three on whom the mantle of Ieuan Gwyllt fell when it came to the conducting of the *Cymanfa Ganu*. For some thirty years after Ieuan Gwyllt's death in 1877 John Thomas was conducting in every part of Wales — for example his biographer says that he conducted 30 events in the first six months of 1882. Ieuan Gwyllt had insisted on the utmost correctness in every detail. John Thomas concentrated on the meaning of the hymn, both of the words and the music. He would read the words through before they were sung, setting the mood for the singing; he would ask the singers to appreciate the chord to which a certain word was to be sung. To him as much as anyone must therefore be attributed a change in the meaning of the *Cymanfa Ganu* movement, from being a gathering to *work* at the music of the congregation to being itself an act of worship, where the success of an occasion lay not in music learnt for future use but in the emotions aroused at the time. J.T. Rees wrote that whereas he had regarded Ieuan Gwyllt as a kind of Moses leading the people out from an Egypt of ignorance, John Thomas was to him Joshua, leading the people to take possession of the promised land. Something of this difference of approach must have been present quite early. In about 1860 John Thomas competed in an *eisteddfod* in Blaencefn and his tune was condemned as being full of "jerks and jigs". This was of course immediately after the publication of Ieuan Gwyllt's great collection of hymn tunes. The winning tune at that *eisteddfod* has been forgotten, but BLAENCEFN has travelled far with its flowing melody and simple architecture growing from the first line.

BLAENCEFN

Emlyn Evans

An altogether bigger figure was David Emlyn Evans (1843-1913). He was born in Castellnewydd Emlyn and was apprenticed as a clothier, a business in which he worked all his life. He had his home for sometime in Hereford where he was a commercial traveller for his employers, combining his work with his overwhelming interest in music in all parts of Wales. He learnt his music from the lesson books then available, and had occasional lessons from Ieuan Gwyllt. He was a successful competitor in the National Eisteddfod for a number of years before turning into a pungent critic of that institution and of the way Wales was lagging behind the rest of Europe musically and above all in failing to produce composers in the great musical forms. He turned from the smaller forms, particularly the glee which was the standard form for competitions in the middle of the century, and composed a number of Cantatas. He was widely respected — not to say feared — as a judge in competitions, since he clearly respected no one if he felt the truth had to be told. He had a hand in the editing of the most important musical periodical of the time, *Y Cerddor* (*The Musician*) from 1880-1913. He was a constant contributor on musical matters to newpapers and periodicals; he shared the editorship of a number of hymn books. He edited and harmonized over 500 traditional Welsh melodies for Nicholas

Bennett's *Alawon fy Ngwlad* (*My Country's Melodies* 1896); he was in demand as a conductor of music festivals and of *Cymanfaoedd Ganu,* though it is clear that if presented with tunes with which he quarrelled he would simply refuse to conduct them. His finest tune is undoubtedly the powerful TREWEN. Its strength derives from a number of elements. The only repetition comes when the melody of the first line brings the tune to a strong conclusion. The stepwise pattern of the first bars becomes the motif used throughout except in the first arpeggio notes of lines five and six, which are strikingly emphasized by their being in unison. The repetition of the same rhythmic pattern throughout, which could be merely boring in some hands, finally gives the tune a hypnotic power. The problem in using this tune outside Wales is in finding words strong enough to sing to it.

TREWEN

David Jenkins

Emlyn Evans brought to his music a thoroughly professional rigour in every aspect. But he was not a professional musician any more than any of those so far mentioned since the great Harpists and John Jones (1725-1796), Organist of St Paul's London. In David Jenkins (1848-1915), the third of the successors to those who brought about the rebirth of Welsh music, we at last come to one such, even though he came to his profession late. He was born in Trecastell, Breckonshire, and because his father died when he was very young he had few early advantages. He was apprenticed as a tailor, but showed that music was his real interest in life. He early became involved in the Tonic Sol-fa movement and showed talent as a composer. In 1874, the year that Joseph Parry arrived a Aberystwyth to take charge of the Music at the College there, he enrolled as a student. He graduated as Bachelor of Music of Cambridge in 1878. When the University of Wales was granted its charter in 1893 he was appointed as lecturer in Music in the newly created Department of Music at Aberystwyth. He became Professor of Music in 1910 and died in office. He was well known in the *eisteddfod* movement and in conducting *Cymanfaoedd Ganu* and he did much to raise the taste of congregations. For many years he was the editor of *Y Cerddor*: he composed a great deal, from small vocal pieces to oratorio and opera.

He wrote many hymntunes. At this time however, as the influences of the world outside Wales came to be felt, there was a particular temptation for the more cultured musicians to follow the styles fashionable in England at the time. This was particularly so in the writing of hymntunes, where the Victorian hymntunes of such composers as John Bacchus Dykes and Joseph Barnby provided a seductive model. The tunes were written for a different situation in the settled congregations of the established church in England. The truly Welsh tunes retain the mood of Revival. David

Jenkin's tunes are by no means as anglicized as some that were being written. But there is something contradictory about them. They are the work of a professional musician and yet musicians are the very people who tend to be unhappy with them. It is of course true beyond Wales that few wholly successful hymn tunes have been composed by professional composers. That is not to say that David Jenkins' tunes are not popular. PENLAN is known outside Wales, having overcome the problem common in Welsh tunes of the feminine endings to lines by being matched to the words 'In heavenly love abiding' — not a strong text. BUILTH is an example of the kind of tune that is very popular in the present day *cymanfa,* but is a little too easy-going for the noise that it engenders.

PENLAN

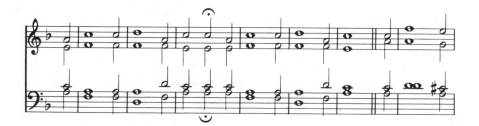

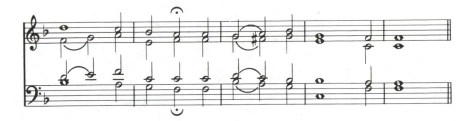

BUILTH

These three were the men that carried on the work of the generation that reconstructed Welsh congregational music. In their hands the results were less severe than with Ieuan Gwyllt. They are better regarded as successors to Tanymarian, the composer of the heart, as it was said, than to Ieuan Gwyllt the composer from the head.

Joseph Parry

But there was another musician in the field, towering above them all, but not as devoted as they to the music of the worshipping congregation. That was Joseph Parry (1841-1903). He was born into a poor family in Merthyr Tydfil; by the age of ten he was working in a coal mine and by twelve in an iron works. As in so many of the industrial towns of the time there was a strong musical culture around him and he sang alto in oratorio performances conducted by Rosser Beynon (see page 181). In 1854 he moved with his family to Dannville, Pennsylvania USA, where he worked in a rolling-mill until 1865. There was a musical class run by other workers and he studied in that. He won a prize for composition in 1860 and as a result his fellow workers subscribed to send him to the college at Genesco, New York. He returned to Wales in 1862 and took a post as organist. He won prizes in the National Eisteddfod in 1863, 1864 and 1866. He returned to America in 1866-7 and as as result of the enthusiasm generated by the concerts he gave, funds were again raised to enable him to return to England to attend the Royal Academy of Music. From there he returned to Dannville where he founded a music school. He was recalled to Wales to take up the post of Head of Music at the newly founded University College at Aberystwyth, a post which he held from 1874 till 1880. In 1878 he was made a Doctor of Music of Cambridge. He ran a private college of music in Aberystwyth from 1879-1881. In that year he moved it to Swansea where from 1881-88 he was also organist of Ebenezer Chapel. In 1888 he moved to University College, Cardiff where he was first lecturer and then Professor of Music until his death in 1903. He was in great demand as an adjudicator and was busy with his students in promoting concerts at which many of his own compositions were performed. He was a very fluent composer, writing operas, oratorios, cantatas, songs, some instrumental music and some 400 hymn tunes. His opera 'Blodwen' received some five hundred performances between 1880 and 1896, and items from it are still regularly heard today. The occasional complete performance of the work proves that he could reproduce at will the styles of many of the great nineteenth century composers. There is however little that is utterly distinctive of himself to hold these styles together and few if any of his works have remained in the repertoire, except a handful of hymn tunes. There is no doubt that the finest of these is ABERYSTWYTH. In his *Autobiography*

Joseph Parry records that it was composed in 1876. It appeared in the *Ail Lyfr Tonau ac Emynau* (1879 *The Second Book of Tunes and Hymns*) of Tanymarian. It does not seem that the composer attached great importance to the tune at the time of its composition, but he did think well enough of it to use it to end his cantata *Ceridwen*. It has proved to be the most widely used of all the Welsh hymn tunes; it gained acceptance in English books well before any others and was included in many books of the first half of the twentieth century where there is no other Welsh tune. It is widely used to Charles Wesley's 'Jesus, Lover of my soul' where its mounting phrases in the second half of the tune, sinking finally to a sombre close admirably match the words. It is through-composed tune, built with all the craft to be expected of a professional composer. The first four lines are confined within the lower fifth of the scale with a strong minor tonality; line five, with a typically unerring Welsh touch, has a bright major tonality; line six begins the climb to higher regions, but with a minor feeling again; line seven reaches the highest note of the tune at its very beginning, with another burst of the same major key, but sinks back to a last line which is a recapitulation of the first. It is a tune that needs to be sung in full harmony with the numerous passing notes in the lower parts being allowed to restrain the pace, so that without becoming sluggish, the words have time to be appreciated with their full power.

ABERYSTWYTH

Every Welsh hymnbook has a selection of Joseph Parry's many tunes. His DIES IRAE (known also as MERTHYR TYDFIL) has appeared in a number of English language books: it is more simple in construction but nevertheless satisfying. Less known outside Wales is SIRIOLDEB (Cheerfulness). It has something of that an-glicized feeling that has already been noted as a danger for Welsh musicians, but its remarkable rhythm in the second line is answering the needs of the Welsh words.

SIRIOLDEB

The final flowering

These were the important names of the great period of Welsh hymn tune composing and indeed singing at the end of the 19th century and the beginning of the 20th. There were many of their contemporaries who were writing tunes. Many of these tunes have become well known in Wales. Some of these composers were important on the wider stage of Welsh music, but few of them were important outside Wales. The best tune seems often to have been the work of a man who, even if he wrote many, wrote only one fine tune. The tunes themselves must therefore be the guide to the composers who receive mention in the final stages of this story. They will be recorded in the order of their dates of birth. The criterion for inclusion will not even be the musical quality of the tunes they composed but whether one of their tunes has proved to have staying power in use.

John Richards (1843-1901, known as 'Isalaw') besides being a minor composer wrote articles on music for journals. As the desire for choral music grew and as Sol-fa became the universally accepted notation for singers in Wales, there was a great demand for all the great oratorios and cantatas, together with the popular anthems and part songs, to be published in that notation. Some Welsh composers also worked in Sol-fa, and their work needed to be available in 'Old Notation' for accompanists. John Richards was well-known as a copyist and transcriber both from and into Sol-fa because of the neatness and precision of his work. His great tune is SANCTUS, always sung to Bishop Mant's hymn 'Bright the vision that delighted' (usually beginning at 'Round the Lord in glory seated') whether in English or in Welsh.

SANCTUS

That is an example of the Welsh tune at its most exuberant. Its heavy, gloomy manifestation, is at its extreme in LLEF (A Cry). Griffiths H. Jones (1849-1919, known as 'Gutyn Arfon') earned his living as a teacher and was both poet and musician, well known for his conducting and his teaching of Sol-fa in North-West Wales. He was the first to bring a musical instrument into a North Wales chapel. This is the preferred tune in many places for Isaac Watts' great hymn 'When I survey the wondrous cross'.

LLEF

216

J.T. Rees was an active musician over a very long life (1857-1949). He was born near Ystradgynlais and was working in a Cwm Rhondda coalmine at the age of nine. He learnt music by means of Tonic Sol-fa. He then went to study with Joseph Parry in Aberystwyth and took the degree of Mus Bac (Toronto). He taught music in America for some years. He composed in many forms for both instruments and voices, He is said to have conducted more *cymanfaoedd ganu* than any other Welshman. He was on the committee for both the 1897 and 1929 Methodist Hymnbooks, and in the latter there are ten arrangements and sixteen original tunes by him. Few are more attractive than LLWYNBEDW (the name of the farmhouse where he was born) in the familiar 878747 metre, which admirably suits the great Ann Griffiths hymn 'Wele'n sefyll rhwng y myrtydd' (There he stands among the myrtles: see page 124).

LLWYNBEDW

Almost as longlived was William Penfro Rowlands, of Maenclochog, Pembrokeshire (1860-1937). He was a school-teacher but also a talented musician. He became the conductor of the Morriston United Choral Society, one of the finest in the country, and was precentor of the Tabernacle Congregational Church there, one of the most famous places in the land for its singing. He is known now only for one tune from his many vocal compositions. BLAENWERN (the name comes from a farm in Pembrokeshire) was composed during the revival of 1904-5 and reflects some of the frenetic excitement of that time. It is probably better known outside Wales than within, and that for the good reason that it is not a vintage Welsh tune. It came into general use when it was included in the songbooks of Billy Graham.

BLAENWERN

That again is an example of an extravert Welsh tune. A complete contrast is CYMER which is the encapsulation of what feels most typically Welsh in the few bars of a Short Metre tune. There is no room for the unison phrases used so powerfully in many tunes, but the single notes in unison are made equally telling in this context of restraint. Lewis Davies (1863-1951) was another schoolmaster; he moved to Cymer, near Port Talbot in 1886 and remained there for the rest of his life, serving the Congregational Church there as elder and church secretary. He was a novelist as well as musician.

CYMER

   Daniel Prothero (1866-1934) was an altogether more colourful figure. He was born in Ystradgynlais. Among his early teachers was J.T.Rees. He had a fine treble voice and won prizes at the National Eisteddfod. By the time he was 19 he was conducting a choir in his home town, but in the following year he moved to Scranton, Pennsylvania. In 1890 he graduated in music (Mus Bac Toronto). He conducted a number of well-known choirs in America, being for many years in charge of the music at Central Church Chicago. He returned to Wales frequently, where he adjudicated at the National Eisteddfod and conducted choral festivals. He composed a great deal for voices. There are a number of his hymn tunes in the Welsh books, not all of them easily distinguishable from English tunes. HIRAETH is one of the great Welsh words, meaning 'longing, nostalgia', the typical feeling of the exile for his homeland, and this tune, with its unusually flexible rhythm, is expressive of that. It therefore picks up the mood of those hymns, common in William Williams, Pantycelyn and in later writers, which express a longing for heaven.

HIRAETH

220

A perfect match in sentimentality is the singing of Elfed's 'Rho i'm yr hedd, na wyr y byd amdano' (Give me the peace that the world knows nothing of) to the tune RHYS. It demands inclusion because it does display the way that the Welsh rhetoric in tune writing can be used to less worthy ends. The composer W.J. Evans (1866-1947) was one of the four music editors of the Congregational hymn book of 1921.

RHYS

Yet another minor composer who composed one very fine tune was Thomas John Williams (1869-1944). Ralph Vaughan Williams was prepared to put EBENEZER among the world's one hundred finest tunes. The date of 1896 was given for its composition in an article on the composer in *Trysorfa'r Plant* (*The Children's Treasury*) of 1940, when the composer was still alive. The composer included it in an anthem 'Golau yn y glyn' (Light in the valley). It became well known during the 1904-5 revival, and from that became known in England. It was first published in a book in the *Baptist Book of Praise* (probably 1901), and it was after its appearance there that the story was spread that it had been found washed up in a bottle on the coast of North Wales. Thus it came to be called TON-Y-BOTEL (The Bottle Tune). The proper name comes in fact from the chapel in Rhos, Pontardawe of which the composer was a member at the time the tune was composed. The triplet movement in the tune is unusual at this period, though there are older tunes that show it (MORIAH and GWALIA). The tune must not be sung too fast; it is by no means a jig. The triplet is sung quite heavily in Welsh and there is no need to distinguish it from the dotted figure elsewhere in the tune. The form of the tune is the common AABA with the B section as so often striking into the major.

EBENEZER

The popularity of EBENEZER alongside ABERYSTWYTH may have built up the widespread impression that all Welsh hymn tunes are in the minor. It is difficult, however, to see how that impression has stood up to the overwhelming popularity of CWM RHONDDA (Rhondda Valley), which for many stands as the archetypal Welsh hymn tune, and which is sturdily in the major. It is again the only piece of any kind by its composer that has come into wide use. John Hughes (1873-1932) was, like so many musicians, a product of the South Wales coal fields, with their harsh conditions alleviated by a vigorous chapel life that in its turn supported a strong musical, above all choral movement. When he was only twelve he started work at the Glynn Colliery at Llanilltyd Faerdref. In 1905 he was appointed clerk at the Great Western Colliery, Pontypridd, where he remained for over forty years. In that same year his most famous tune was sung at the Baptist *Cymanfa Ganu,* Pontypridd, for which it was written. He was active as a deacon and leader of the singing with the Baptists throughout his life, and a number of his other compositions were popular for a while. CWM RHONDDA was resisted by the main hymn book editors in both Welsh and English for many years, no doubt because of the tune's great vigour and, what can best be called its vulgar appeal — not necessarily a bad thing in a hymn. It is invariably in English matched with William Williams Pantycelyn's great pilgrimage hymn 'Guide me, O thou great Jehovah/Redeemer'. It should be sung for its full worth, in harmony, and not too fast, with the bass striding through the first four lines and rising, with the repetition of the words in both bass and alto, to the dominant seventh chord at the end of the fifth line. It is sad to see editors trying to edit away these elements from a tune which may not be a classic, but which has its own qualities. It is even more sad to find that, though it is not often used in Wales, least of all for the original of the William Williams' hymn, it is the almost invariable choice for Ann Griffiths' great love song to her Saviour 'Wele'n sefyll rhwng y myrtwydd', which has nothing to do with CWM RHONDDA's martial tread.

CWM RHONDDA

By contrast David Evans (1874-1948) lived a very distinguished and useful life as an academic and church musician, and as a leader of Welsh national musical life. Yet he left no single tune that sets him undisputably among the angels. He was born in Resolven, Glamorgan and had a sound education, studying at Arnold College, Swansea and University College Cardiff under Joseph Parry. He took a Mus Bac at Oxford in 1895, and later the D Mus. He was from 1899-1903 Organist and Choirmaster at one of the great London Welsh Chapels, Jewin Street Presbyterian. From 1903 he was lecturer and head of music at University College, Cardiff and when in 1908 the chair was founded he became Professor, a post he retained until 1939. He was a considerable influence on the music of Wales chiefly through his teaching, but also through his adjudications at the National Eisteddfod, his own compositions and through his editorship of *Y Cerddor* from 1916-21. He published a collection of standard hymn tunes *Moliant Cenedl* (*A Nation's Praise*). He took up the cause of the *Cymanfa Ganu* and was in great demand as a conductor. He was the chief musical editor of *The Revised Church Hymnary* 1927, of the Church of Scotland and he edited the music of *Llyfr Emynau a Thonau* (1929, *The Book of Hymns and Tunes,* the joint Hymn Book of the Calvinistic and Wesleyan Methodists, and probably still the best collection of Welsh hymn tunes). Both books contain a number of his arrangements of tunes, many of which have been taken over into other books. He wrote a number of tunes both under his own name and as 'Edward Arthur'. They all have a very strong English flavour. LUCERNA LAUDONIAE, for example, a delightful tune for the words 'For the beauty of the earth', seems strongly influenced by English folksong. Erik Routley comments that his tune YN Y GLYN (In the Valley) 'reads like a good imitation of a Welsh tune composed by an Englishman'. It was in fact written in memory of none other than John Thomas, Llanwyrtyd, David Evans' great predecessor as the leading conductor in his day of the *cymanfaoedd ganu.*

YN Y GLYN

The story of Caradog Roberts (1878-1935) is a reminder that even in the last quarter of the 19th century it was not easy to get a musical education. He showed his musical talents early, but nevertheless was first a student-teacher in an elementary school and then was apprenticed for three years as a carpenter. He was noticed by Dr. Roland Roberts, organist of Chester Cathedral, as an organist, and by the singer and composer William Davies as an accompanist. It is clear that he was an extraordinarily fluent keyboard player. Thereafter he had good lessons, from the organists both of Chester and Liverpool Cathedrals. He excelled in academic studies also and graduated B Mus externally at Oxford in 1906. In 1911 he gained the Oxford D Mus with the traditional composition exercise in the form of an oratorio for soloists, double-choir and full orchestra. Having held posts elsewhere he returned in 1904 to his native place as Organist and Choirmaster of Bethlehem Congregational Chapel, Rhosllanerchrugog, Denbighshire, not far from Wrexham. That was his home till his death and he became more and more of a folk-hero there. He was part-time music organizer of the University College, Bangor; he travelled far and wide as conductor of *cymanfaoedd ganu,* adjudicator at *eisteddfodau,* organist and above all as as choral conductor. His compositions were many, but he lacked originality and the will to break out of the 19th century tradition of the oratorio after the fashion of Mendelssohn. His style, even in his hymn tunes, is anglicized, following the weaker models of such hymn books as *Ancient and Modern.* One of his tunes RACHIE, written as a children's hymn but now more often sung to the words of a temperance hymn is very popular in Wales, being sung socially perhaps more often than in worship; it has appeared in English books to 'Who is on the Lord's side'. IN MEMORIAM is the only tune that rises to the heights, with a distinctive Welsh feel to it, probably because it is written, as the name shows, in memory of a famous choral conductor, Harry Evans (1873-1914). Its most distinctive feature lies in the third chord of the tune and in the way that an expectation is built up that in every line the third chord is going to be distinctive. This is heightened in lines five, six and seven by the first two notes being in unison, and the expectation is rewarded in line seven by the high major chord with no discord that provides the tune's climax, after which it sinks to a close with a skilfully contrived repeat of the first line (the same feature as is to be found in TREWEN and ABERYSTWYTH). For the first time this is a tune that demands to by analyzed by its harmony rather than by its melody. Full-blown four-part singing had by this time become part of the Welsh composer's background; but the hymntune was so much a folk art that it rarely lost its emphasis on melody.

IN MEMORIAM

T. Osborne Roberts (1879-1948) was a much more local figure in North Wales. He moved to Ysbyty Ifan on the upper reaches of the Conway River when he was twelve. He worked in the office of a large estate for a while, but at the beginning of this century moved to Llandudno and took up music full time. He was organist in Llandudno and then in Caernarvon, and was known as a local adjudicator and conductor. His best known tune is PEN-

NANT. The rhythm, which on its own may seem a little monotonous, takes up the rhythm of the words in this metre. Its distinctive feature is the way that the opening unison phrase is harmonized on its reappearances.

PENNANT

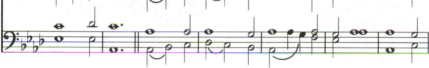

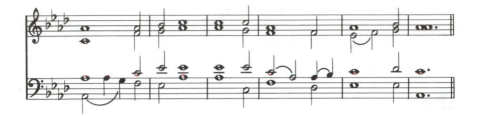

It is clear that during the last half of the 19th century and the first years of the twentieth many if not most of the best tunes were written in the first place not with the local congregation in mind but the *cymanfa ganu,* with its larger numbers and its more disciplined singing under a conductor. Some of the signs of this are soaring tenor parts, melodies that leap about much more than is normal in a congregational tune, and pauses, often at the end of the last line but one, where the conductor can take control. Much of this can be seen in BRYN MYRDDIN by J. Morgan Nichols (1895-1963).

BRYN MYRDDIN

The tunes of John Hughes (1896-1968) and his brother Arwel Hughes (1909-1988) are more smoothly crafted than many of those that went before. This, though admirable in one respect, can be seen as a sign of the decline in the hymn culture that followed the first World War. The *cymanfa ganu* became more and more isolated from the realities of church life. Congregations were falling away ever more inexorably and the numbers of those speaking Welsh diminishing ever more rapidly first as a result of social and economic pressures and then in the face of the influence of radio and finally of television. John Hughes began by studying music in his spare time as a miner in Hafod Colliery in Denbighshire. He went eventually to University College, Aberystwyth where he graduated in 1924. He was organist and choirmaster in Treorci before being appointed Music Organizer for Meirionethshire Education Authority. *Y Llawlyfr Moliant Newydd* (1956, *The New Handbook of Praise,* the Baptist Hymn Book) shows his skill and taste as music editor, as does the English *Baptist Hymn Book* where he was prominent on the music committee. His early tune MAELOR has some of the sternness that Ieuan Gwyllt would have appreciated, while giving interesting parts to bass and tenor.

MAELOR

ARWELFA is a different matter. An interesting comparison can be made between it and BLAENWERN. The earlier tune is rough by comparison; the later one might even be an unconscious reworking of it, so similar are they in shape. ARWELFA has an easy mastery, but sung as it often is to words that express a mutual satisfaction at being together on the way to the heavenly land it has an inward-looking feeling. In these circumstances it has an air of decadence.

ARWELFA

Arwel Hughes was mainly a secular musician, though he did play the organ at the Tabernacle Chapel, The Hayes, Cardiff. He was for many years the head of the Music Department of the British Broadcasting Corporation in Wales and conductor of the BBC Welsh Orchestra. His best known contribution as a composer is the oratorio *Dewi Sant* (*Saint David* 1961). His only contribution to the hymn repertoire can hardly be considered a congregational hymn, though it is in much demand on other occasions. It is a setting of a rather slight devotional poem, the first words of which give the tune its name TYDI A RODDAIST ('Tis thou didst give the dawn its hue). The tune feels as though it comes to a premature end: the unison phrase gives the impression that there are four more lines to come. Then after verse three, all is revealed in the final extended 'Amen' where the conductor of the *cymanfa ganu* can urge his tenors to their top 'G' and his sopranos to their top 'A'.

TYDI A RODDAIST

233

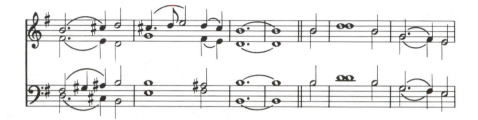

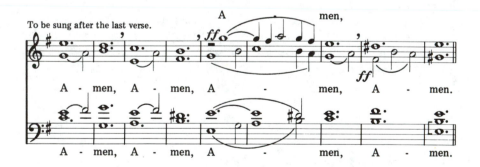

Arwel Hughes must have been the name that Erik Routley missed when he wrote that none of the composers in *Llawlyfr Moliant Newydd* (1956) were born after 1900. The observation has its point however. There have been good musicians writing tunes, but there has been no really new writing of hymn texts to take them forward. There have been many fine musicians in Wales in this century, but their work is concentrated outside the churches. It is just possible that at one point there may have been a musical impetus which might have led to new developments. It is doubtful whether it could have achieved anything however without new words, and in any case the promise was cut off tragically early. For there is one name missing from this roll-call, that of the greatly gifted woman composer Morfydd Llwyn Owen (1891-1918). She was born in Treforest, Glamorgan, of musically gifted parents and studied music first at University College, Cardiff (1909-12) under David Evans, and then at the Royal Academy of Music, London (1912-17), where she took a number of the chief prizes. She was outstanding as singer and pianist, but above all as a composer. She had already written a number of fine pieces by her death, for orchestra, as well as songs and choral pieces. She wrote three hymn tunes: RICHARD, WILLIAM and PENUCHA. The first two are quite severe and masterly in the particularly Welsh metres of 8787 (the Welsh psalm meter) and 288888 (the BRAINT meter). The third is in 888.888 for which there are few good tunes in any repertoire. The problem in using the tune outside Wales is that it is so powerful that it needs equally powerful words to match it. Isaac Watts' 'I'll praise my maker while I've breath' is a good candidate. What is usually found striking about the tune is its modulation. The modulation however comes from the economy and logic of the melody, the whole being built from the *motif* of the first line and the descending phrase that makes lines three and six. The unison voices have never been used with more power than here in the last line, vocally (all starting on the top 'E') or musically, with the accompanying harmonies in support. But the final stroke of genius is the small one of the insistent pair of crotchets (quarter notes) at only two pitches throughout the tune despite its modulation and always on the sixth syllable of the line. This is a tune of genius. Though other tunes may have followed in point of time, this is the last word so far, musically, in the long history of the Welsh HymnTune.

PEN UCHA

What is the Welsh Hymntune?

Musically the Welsh hymntune is the result of the development of the musical style of the 18th century. There is nothing
archaic about it. The tunes are, except one, BRAINT (see Example
152), in the major or minor of the musical orthodoxy of the
century and a half over which the style grew. There are some roots

in the native ballad and carol tradition, but the meters of the tunes owe more to the hymns of the 18th century Evangelical Revival in England which were used as models. The style owes nothing directly to the folksongs and national melodies of Wales. Indeed the leaders of the Revival tried to banish such things from the minds of their converts. But such things do not die easily and the influence of these secular melodies was present all around to haunt the imagination of those who were composing the new hymntunes.

The use that is made of the major and minor modes is simple enough. When in the major the Welsh tunes often make use of the notes of the major triads of the key, while in the minor a stepwise motion is more common. This is not to say anything very profound or distinctive of Wales. All the strongest and most memorable tunes are built by a careful juxtaposition of leaps and stepwise motion. DARWALL'S 148th is a classic of this in the English repertoire: LLANFAIR is a classic example in the Welsh, first striding up the major chord, repeating notes for emphasis on the way and then twice cascading down by steps once the top has been reached (see page 169). The variation works the other way in TREWEN, where, true to the tendency in minor mode tunes, the movement is by steps to begin with; this continues for four lines and then lines five and seven begin with downward arpeggio phrases, making a powerful contrast (see page 208).

The form of the tunes is usually conventional, and much indebted to the ballad tradition and to the earlier English tunes. AABA is a common pattern in all tune-making, and it is found over and over again in the earlier Welsh tunes of eight lines. Even among these early tunes there can be some sophistication, with the final A being developed (AABA', see MEIRIONYDD page 174) or with the second A being somewhat developed and then used to end the tune (AA'BA', see LLANGLOFFAN page 160). HYFRYDOL (see page 177) uses a quite different technique again, by building up the expectation that the tune is to be AABA and in fact ending with something quite different (AABC). All the possible variants can be found with some of the finest tunes being through-composed.

There are some points that are imitated over and over again. There is a tendency for a contrasting section to move to a different part of the voice, making the effect more marked (see DINIWEIDRWYDD page 153). In minor mode tunes the composer or arranger will often move briefly into the major at some point during the tune, even though it would be perfectly possible to remain in the minor.

All these points however do not create a recipe for writing a tune that will sound Welsh. Many of the tunes by Welsh composers, especially in the later years of the 19th century and the early years of the twentieth use all these techniques and have nothing distinctively Welsh about them. In fact the more cultivated the Welsh musicians became the more likely this was to happen. The finest and most distinctively Welsh tunes are distinguished by their expression of a particular religious zeal in a musical rhetoric that the composers could share with those who would use the hymns. The best Welsh tunes are those by composers who were in touch with their roots, spiritually, nationally and linguistically. They are essentially folksong even though we know who wrote them. They are written within a community of worship for a particular kind of usage, and the older tunes are re-worked to be part of that. At its height this usage gained the huge advantage of a system of music notation in Tonic Sol-fa that enabled the whole congregation to sing their vocal part. It is not music to be performed for an audience: it is music for participation, and every choral conductor knows that there is the world of difference between listening to a choir and joining with it. As soon as the singer's voice is ringing in his or her own head, all the other voices gain in beauty and blend. So a chapel full of people can be lifted to a kind of ecstasy by their own singing, and often is.

As the kind of religious life that produced these composers and their tunes disappears so does the likelihood that this phenomenon will repeat itself. The tunes, however, remain, and at least for the moment it is still possible to hear the singing in Wales on its native ground. There is the potential in Wales for a similar growth to happen again. It will not be the same as before, just as it seems unlikely that the churches of Wales will be moved by the Spirit in the same way that they were moved for over a century and a half following the great awakening. When the new movement in Welsh hymnody comes, it will not be for our benefit who observe from outside. As with this first growth it will come from a desire to worship God from within the experience of a particular people at a particular time, for that finally was what produced the Welsh hymns.

Appendix

THE PRONUNCIATION OF WELSH

The pronunciation of Welsh is quite consistent, unlike English in its various versions throughout the world. There are twenty simple letters in the alphabet and seven double letters.

Those willing to make the attempt to get near the original sound especially of the names of the tunes will need to master a few basic differences between the English and Welsh spelling and sounds.

Refining the pronounciation beyond that is more difficult, but a beginner's guide is given.

1. Basic differences

There are some traps which should be noted first:

ll is a consonant unique to Welsh, but so common, especially in place names, that it is worth trying to master it. Place the tongue against the roof of the mouth behind the top teeth, as for an ordinary 'l', and blow. The sound may come out on both sides of the tongue or only one. The native Welsh sound 'll' both ways. Remember that it is a sound from the front of the mouth, not the back.

f is pronounced as 'v' as in 'of'. **ff** is pronounced without voicing it, as in 'off'. Simply remember 'of' and 'off'. So the name 'Ifor' is exactly the same name as 'Ivor' (though the Welsh would make a different sound on the 'I' making it nearer 'Eevor'.)

dd is a quite specific sound in Welsh, that of the English voiced 'th' as in 'the'. It never functions as a double 'd' as in the English 'wedded'.

w is in Welsh a vowel with the value of 'oo'. It may, however be either long or short. Thus 'cwm' (a closed valley) has the 'oo' sound as in 'foot'.

Most Welsh words are accented or stressed on the last syllable but one. Failure to observe this rule will make a word sound very un-Welsh.

2. The Vowels

The Vowels have their European continental values, as in German or Italian. They do not change shape as they are spoken; they are kept pure. Even the

English equivalents given below can be misleading in some regional forms of speech.

a is always 'ah' never 'ay': when it is long as it is in 'father' when short it is as in 'rat'.

e is as in 'bed'.

i is, when long, a straight sound as in 'machine'; when it is short it is the same sound, as in a word such as 'been' when it is unaccented in a sentence; it is never as in 'bin'.

o is always an open sound and tends, whether long or short, towards the sound as in 'not', and is never as in 'tone'.

y may have two sounds according to its place in the word. In one both **u** and **y** have the same sound; in South Wales this is the same as the 'i' sound. In North Wales it is nearer the French 'u' or the German 'ü'.

At other times the **y** has a sound very close to the vowel in 'the'. This its sound in the definite article 'Y'. This is the only ambiguity in Welsh spelling.

w is a vowel equivalent to 'oo' as in 'food' (see above).

Both 'i' and 'w' may begin a word in which case they function rather like consonants as in English.

The combination **wy** is often found and is a dipthong. (This contributes to the feeling that many Welsh words have no vowels) The word 'gwyn' is pronounced 'win' with the 'g' placed in front.

There are many other combinations of Welsh vowels; their definition is a complicated matter and would serve little purpose in this basic guide.

3. The Consonants

Single (sounding usually exactly as in English; a consonant however, may have two sounds in English whereas it will have only one of those sounds in Welsh).

p and **b** are sounded as in English.

t and **d** are sounded as in English.

c and **g** are sounded as in the English hard forms, 'k' and 'g' as in 'get'. They are never sounded as 's' and 'j'.

m and **n** are sounded as in English.

l is sounded as in English.

r should if possible be trilled.

s has the sound of the English as in 'cost'; it is never 'z' as in 'cosy'.

h has the sound of the English aspirate. It is never dropped.

i and **w** may act as consonants (see above).

Double (taking their place in the alphabet as letters in their own right; this needs to be remembered when using Welsh indexes)

ff and **ph** have the same sound (see above).

dd has the sound of the voiced 'th' in English, as in 'the' (see above).

ch has the sound of the 'ch' in the Scotch 'loch' or in the German 'nacht'.

ll is officially described as 'a voiceless unilateral 'l' ' (see above).

ng has the sound of 'ng' in 'song', but may appear at the beginning of a word.

mh, nh and **ngh** do not appear in the alphabet, but are combinations that appear at the beginning of words. They are unvoiced: the basic consonant is formed, after which there is a strong aspirate.

In general Welsh is pronounced more distinctly than English, with very few syllables dropped or swallowed.

INDEXES

The entries are indexed according to the conventions of English spelling and not Welsh. Thus 'LL' is indexed as if two letters and not as a single letter as would be proper in Welsh.

1.
HYMN AND OTHER TUNES

(Hymn tunes are given in capitals: bold type indicates that the complete tune is given.)

ABERYSTWYTH 130, 212, **213**, 222, 227
ALMAEN 175
ARFON 151-2
ALEXANDER 184
ALL THROUGH THE NIGHT 28, 130
AR HYD Y NOS 28,130
Ar gyfer heddiw fore **36**
ARWELFA **232**
ASH GROVE **27**, 29, 130
Awn i Fethlem **34**, 137

BETHEL 157
Black eyed Susan 34
BLAENCEFN **206**
BLAENWERN **218**, 232
BRAINT **152**, 161, 235
BRYN CALFARIA 130, **183**
BRYNHYFRYD **163**
BRYN MYRDDIN **230**
BUILTH 210, **211**

CAERLLEON **142**
CAERLLYGOED 193
CAERSALEM **170**
CALCUTTA 175
Can love be controlled by advice 143, **144**
Can mlynedd i nawr 154
Can mlynedd yn ôl 154
CAPEL Y DDOL **181**
CEMAES 163
Charity Mistress 34
Charming Chloe 34
CLOD **143**

Come, open the door, sweet Betty 142
CRUGYBAR 130, **157**
CWM RHONDDA 130, 223, **224**
CYFAMOD 143, **146**, 157
CYMER **219**
Cysga di fy mhlentyn dlws **33**

DARWALLS'S 148th 237
David of the white rock 28
DEAD MARCH IN SAUL 195
Death and the Lady 142
DEVIZES 175
DEWCH I'R FRWYDR 139
DIES IRAE 214
DIFYRRWCH GWYR Y GOGLEDD 147
DINIWEIDRWYDD **153**, 193, 237
DORCAS 171
DUNDEE 131
DYFFRYN BACA **185**
DYFFRYN SILOAH 163
DYFRDWY 150

EBENEZER 130, 221, **222**
EDINBURGH **156**
EIFIONYDD 179
ELIOT **164**

Fashionable Lady 142
Ffarwel Ned Puw **38**
FFIGYSBREN **143**

Gee ceffyl bach **33**
GELOBT SEI GOTT 150

2.
HYMN AND CAROL TEXTS

(There are listed here texts that are quoted at least at the length of one stanza, together with the corresponding Welsh first line.)

3.
NAMES

4.
GENERAL